BE 1% BETTER

RON CLARK

RON CLARK

BE 1% BETTER

SURPRISINGLY SIMPLE WAYS TO TRANSFORM YOUR SCHOOL

Be 1% Better: Surprisingly Simple Ways to Transform Your School
© 2024 Ron Clark

This book is available at special discounts when purchased in quantity for educational purposes or for use as premiums, promotions, or fundraisers. For inquiries and details, contact the publisher at books@daveburgessconsulting.com.

Published by Dave Burgess Consulting, Inc.
Vancouver, WA
DaveBurgessConsulting.com

Library of Congress Control Number: 2024939082
Paperback ISBN: 978-1-956306-77-4
Hardcover ISBN: 978-1-956306-79-8
Ebook ISBN: 978-1-956306-78-1

Cover and interior design by Liz Schreiter
Edited and produced by Reading List Editorial
ReadingListEditorial.com

To Zyan Wynn
I am eternally proud of you.
Here's to the one percents you will make in countless lives during your teaching career, which I hope will include many memorable games of Connect Four.
Enjoy the journey.

CONTENTS

FOREWORD

Did you miss it?

I would absolutely forgive you if you did.

It's easy to be distracted by the legend of Ron Clark. After all, the man is an icon in the educational world. He is a *New York Times*–best-selling author whose books have made a huge impact. He was played by the late *Friends* star Matthew Perry in a movie made about his early teaching career. He has been on *The Oprah Winfrey Show*. He was named American Teacher of the Year by Disney in 2000. He is a highly sought-after keynote speaker who has transfixed and transformed audiences with his charismatic style. He cofounded and runs one of the most acclaimed teaching academies in the world. The Ron Clark Academy is not only a fully functioning school with students from all walks of life but also a demonstration school where thousands of teachers come each year to watch and learn from the staff and experience professional development in an authentic and powerful way. The classrooms actually have stadium seating for educators to observe from! It has secret passageways and the legendary blue slide where countless teachers have become "slide certified." It is *literally* referred to as the Hogwarts of teaching. I mean, come on—the guy was even on season 38 of *Survivor*!

And that's why so many miss what's perhaps the most essential part of the story.

Ron is a teacher. Not past tense. Still to this very day, while also leading the school, he teaches classes at the Ron Clark Academy, standing and delivering instruction every week of the school year. He is still in the trenches. He taught through the pandemic. He went through the incredible challenges all educators faced in the aftermath as schools reopened and welcomed back students who had been traumatized in many different ways. As I type this, he is prepping his room and curriculum, getting ready for yet another year of building rapport with students while delivering high-quality lessons and changing lives. How many so-called (and I hate this term) "edu-celebrities" are still in the classroom? Spoiler alert: Not me! The man has street cred.

Now, in his first education-focused book in over a decade, Ron reveals the power of creating a one percent better mindset. Don't be fooled by that one percent, though. In the introduction alone, he reveals a life-changing paradigm shift that took him from rookie educator to award-winning, nationally recognized teacher. In the subsequent chapters, he shows surprisingly simple ideas that will flat-out make school better for students, staff, and parents.

Why is the concept of *Be 1% Better* so powerful?

One percent is doable. Right now. This year. This week. You can wrap your mind around one percent. Even the most overwhelmed educator can rise to the call of improving some part of their practice by one percent. The first-year teacher won't be intimidated by a one percent challenge. Equally important, the best and most experienced educators in your system surely have to admit that they, too, can find something to make one percent better. If you talk to a new teacher, an overwhelmed teacher, or even the superstar teacher on your staff about transforming everything they do or making giant shifts in their practices, you are headed for poor morale and—most likely—poor results. One percent, though? Let's go!

The fact that these one percent changes require only a small initial lift also encourages staff to try new things and take risks. Why not try that new idea? What's the worst that can happen? It's only a one percent effort. If it doesn't work out, just iterate and try again. When we make an enormous investment in time and energy, we are less likely to be willing to shift course. It's the sunk cost fallacy: the bigger the investment we've made—whether it's in time, energy, money, or even creative thought—the less likely we are to recognize and accept the need to change. That's the underrated power of small change. We can truly embrace innovation through iteration when we are able to effortlessly abandon failed ideas.

And it works for every single stakeholder in your system. Teachers can be one percent better. School leadership can shift one percent. The support staff can do it. The custodial team can find a one percent better idea to embrace. Parents and students, too. It is a school culture initiative that is truly universal, and no initiative effectively works on the system level without buy-in from all corners.

So, sure, you are going to find some exciting ideas here from Ron and a whole cadre of incredible contributors that will allow you to improve your practice in meaningful ways. But you'll find the real power of this book when you and your colleagues brainstorm your very own special and unique ways to do what Ron Clark shows so well: make the unwavering commitment to be one percent better.

—**Dave Burgess,** author of *Teach Like a Pirate* and president of Dave Burgess Consulting, Inc.

INTRODUCTION

Ronnie Martin was playing probably the worst game of basketball in his life; every time he touched the ball, instead of shooting or passing, he'd look over to see if I was still watching.

Ronnie never expected to see me at his game. I hadn't been teaching him long—I hadn't been teaching *anyone* long back then; I was a true rookie—but I'd decided I needed to take extra steps to connect with my students. Ronnie had the worst discipline issues in my class, so I went to his basketball game.

Finally, at halftime, he ran over and did another double take as he looked at me.

"Mr. Clark, what are you doing here?"

"I came to cheer for you," I said.

"You're here to cheer for me?" Ronnie wasn't sure he believed it.

"Yeah, buddy. I don't know these other kids. I'm here to cheer for you."

The ref's whistle blew, but Ronnie kept staring at me, processing what my presence at his game meant while the ball bounced behind him.

When he walked into class that next Monday, Ronnie asked loudly, so that the entire class could hear, "Mr. Clark, you saw those skills, right? You saw those skills?" I told the class how great he'd played, and Ronnie glowed.

Sure, he still had discipline problems sometimes, but whenever he'd start up, I'd ask, "Ronnie, what are you thinking?" He'd pause and say, "Sorry, sir," or "My bad." And I thought to myself, "I'll gladly take it!" Attending their game on a Saturday afternoon won't make children perfect, but it does go a long way to building relationships and improving behaviors.

Teachers know that we must always ask how we can *continue* to improve. Dropping by extracurricular activities, visiting students at home, spending summers and weekends planning lessons, building a school culture around students' voice and choice, spending extra on exciting school trips, and investing in our kids by giving them the tools they need to succeed and setting high expectations—I don't need to tell you all these efforts can take a lot of extra time from each day.

And of course they are worth it, but those efforts can be exhausting and overwhelming.

But even when we're already using all the tricks in our teaching toolboxes, reeling from the fallout of an international pandemic, dealing with discipline problems and disgruntled parents, and facing a nationwide learning-loss crisis, we still have to find ways to strive to be better.

Years after attending Ronnie's game, when I was running the school we founded in Atlanta, the Ron Clark Academy, I had to ask myself that very question when planning an annual staff retreat: How can we continue to improve when we're already giving our all?

It was the end of the pandemic, and my staff had experienced a rapid, trying immersion into remote learning while working overtime to maintain connections with stressed students and overwhelmed parents. Everyone was exhausted. If I had walked into that meeting and said, "We have to be ten times better. Do more, give more, and work harder," the team would have slid beneath the table.

Instead, I explained that we were going to try to be baby steps better. I asked everyone to think about their daily tasks and then ask themselves, "How can I use common sense and dedication to my role to be one percent better at what I do? How can I improve in a way that isn't stressful, overwhelming, or taxing?"

Today, teachers face a world I could scarcely have imagined when I was a kid. I grew up in the 1970s, down country dirt roads in North Carolina, spending my time climbing trees and smelling honeysuckles. Even now, when I open my mouth, a tractor falls out. On our family farm, everyone pitched in to get the crops harvested, digging potatoes by hand. When I was seven, I'd sit by myself all day beside busy Highway 17, just waiting and hoping somebody would come buy a bushel of potatoes for $2.50. No phones, no social media. I just sat alone with my thoughts, which gave me an opportunity to wonder and dream about seeing the world.

Years later, I was the first person in my family to attend college, and while there I worked forty hours a week running a Dunkin' Donuts drive-through. After I had graduated from East Carolina University, my mom told me about an open teaching job—a teacher at a local school had just passed away. I had no interest in teaching, but my mom twisted my arm. When I met with the school's principal, she told me the class had all kinds of kids—ADHD, ADD, and even some "B-A-D" kids. She said, "You're just the man for the job." I replied, "No, I'm not," and she looked shocked as she asked, "Then why are you here?" I sheepishly replied, "Because my mama made me come."

The principal, Mrs. Robinson, asked if she could at least introduce me to the students. I agreed. Now, this is back when teachers forced kids to put their noses and fingers in circles drawn on the chalkboard as a punishment, and when I looked in the class, I saw three kids stuck to the board like that. There was a stressed-out substitute teacher trying to teach, her wig skewed to one side. One of the kids looked up at me and asked, "Is you going to be our new teacher?"

Maybe because of all that time I spent wondering and dreaming on the side of the road, one of my mottoes is "If you get an opportunity to do something, do it." I feel like life is a blessing, and if we don't live our lives to the fullest, we are denying our blessings, so whenever possible, I tell myself, "GO FOR IT. LIVE!" So when that kid asked if I'd be their new teacher, I thought, "Oh my, here we go." I said, "I think so," and Mrs. Robinson grabbed my arm and exclaimed, "You'll take the job," and I just answered, "I guess so."

The next day, I quickly realized I had my hands full. The kids had a lot of discipline problems, but I tried to make learning fun and bring each lesson to life. It took a while to figure out how, because I didn't know yet how much extra you have to give. I was teaching about World Wars I and II with a Venn diagram, and the kids were beyond bored!

Eventually, I changed tactics and created my first-ever learning chant.

"Repeat after me," I sang. "World War I."

"World War I," they replied, with much less energy than I had displayed.

"1914 to 1918. World War II." I continued my little jingle.

"World War II," they responded.

"1939 to 1945," I said.

Honestly, the kids didn't seem that interested. But at lunch the next day, I was eating with the kids (always eat with the kids who have discipline problems—they're funny at lunch!), and from the other end of the table, I heard kids singing, "1914 to 1918."

I sat up straight like a peacock. "They remember my song!" Later, when I graded the test, all the kids got the years right: 1914–1918, 1939–1945. I thought that was incredible. Now, they missed all the other stuff, so I decided to put as much of the content as possible to music. Years before *Hamilton*, I was singing: "Now let's get down to some presidential learning. We'll start with George Washington straight from Mount Vernon. The first president and commander and

4

chief fought the Revolutionary Wars so we can be free. John Adams second, Thomas Jefferson third. When he fought for independence, the voices were heard."

Another student of mine that year, a kid who bullied others, struggled with reading. I began tutoring him one-on-one by helping him practice reading a specific paragraph. Then when we got to that paragraph in class one day, I had him read it aloud. He read it well, and other kids saw him differently. I think he saw himself differently—he relaxed. He whispered to me after class, "Can we do some more of those paragraphs?" and I gladly responded, "Of course!" The more he read, the less he bullied others.

And while he wasn't a good reader yet, now he wanted to be.

There was another girl that year who struggled with math. I sat with her at lunch one day and asked her if she knew what nine times nine times nine was. She said to me in a snotty and defensive tone, "No." I said, "Well, let's work it out." We solved the problem, and I said, "Look, it's 729. Seven and twenty-nine. Seven, two, and nine. 729."

Later that day, in the middle of our math lesson, the problem came up. I asked if anyone knew what nine times nine times nine was. And she piped up, "729."

"Ooh," I said. "You have a good math mind. Y'all, that's the valedictorian! You are sharp!" She had always been such a discipline problem during math class, she would never focus. Once I started giving her the answers, her eyes stayed focused on me the whole time, almost bugging out of her head, and she waited for the moment she would know the answer in math class, a subject she previously hated.

At the end of the year, my test scores were so high that Mrs. Robinson came running down the hall to show them to me. When she asked how I did it, I honestly couldn't really explain what I was doing. I was just acting on instinct. So, for the first time, I started consciously analyzing the strategies I was using, and of all of the tactics I was trying, there was one that I found made the biggest difference in student success and improved test scores. I have now continued to do this for over thirty years with the same level of success. Basically, each year I look at my class of thirty kids. I find the brightest kid in the class, and challenging that child becomes my main goal. My lesson plans are all for that kid—my questions, my hands-on activities. I try to figure out how I can get this kid to truly love the subject matter. My concept is to teach to this gifted kid, challenge this kid every day, and truly push them to achieve greatness.

But the key is, as you teach to the gifted kid, you also need to work hard to engage all of the other students and get them up to that level as well. That's why I use music, movement, balloons, and all kinds of stuff to hold kids' attention and get them up to that level. Of course, I always stop and answer a question if a student of mine asks one. But rather than spending fifteen minutes to explain something they missed because they were bored or disengaged, I keep the whole class moving through active, constant engagement.

People ask, "What if you have kids with learning disabilities?" I feel that teaching "down" to any student's level is doing a disservice to them. The world's not going to make these kids' jobs easier when they grow up, so we need to work harder to prepare all of our students. We must have high expectations for every kid, but we must also try different roads until we can help each kid meet those expectations. That also means we must challenge gifted kids when they are coasting and school seems too simple or easy for them. If we don't push these kids, when something does get hard—in college or the real world—they fall apart.

After teaching like that in North Carolina for five years and being invited to the White House three different times to be honored for our programs, I began to wonder about moving on to see if the methods I was using could work elsewhere. One night, I saw a TV show about schools in Harlem that dealt with violence and overcrowded classrooms. I thought, "Well, I know these things work in the country. Maybe I should go see if they work in the city." I had a strong feeling in my heart, so I drove up to Harlem, found one of the schools that was facing these challenges, and begged for a job. I used the same method I used in North Carolina—I taught to the brightest kid, helping them get an education in which they were challenged, and I made sure class was fun, active, and engaging. I built relationships with every student; I visited their homes and ate lunch with them and worked overtime to create surprises. And in turn, I had the same success with test scores there.

From there, things got wild. TNT made a movie about me teaching in Harlem, starring Matthew Perry. I was named the Disney American Teacher of the Year, I wrote a book, and I got to be on *The Oprah Winfrey Show*. All that dreaming I did as a kid sitting by the roadside with my bushels of potatoes was beginning to pay off.

I knew I wanted to expand and rethink how teachers understood our classroom habits, and I knew that when teachers could see methods that worked firsthand, it made a difference. Suddenly, I had that feeling again. I had an opportunity to do something, and I took a big leap.

I found an old factory in the downtown area of Atlanta. That neighborhood had the second-highest crime rate in the city, but I said, "We're going to put classrooms in this building, and then we're going to teach. In all our classes, we'll find the gifted kid, teach to that kid, and fire everyone up and keep them engaged to get to that level. I want to show how, by doing this, you increase the test scores of kids with learning disabilities, you increase the average kids' scores, and you increase the gifted kids' test scores. And everyone has a better understanding of the content." That old factory is where we built the Ron Clark Academy.

The building cost $840,000, and the book I'd written had made exactly that much. My staff and I relied on donors to create classrooms and buy desks and carpets and supplies. Today, that building is unrecognizable. Our school is beautiful and cool! The whole focus is to be a center of innovation, a center for creativity. There are flying dragons, trapdoors, and secret passageways. Tens of thousands of teachers come from all over the world each year to watch our teachers teach, learn our methods and techniques, and take what we do back to their schools. Schools that were struggling, that were going to be taken over by the state, replicate our methods and are turned around. Teachers who have said they were going to leave the profession have come to our school and then, after implementing our methods, been named as state teachers of the year. We were truly changing schools, helping teachers, and affecting children everywhere.

And then the pandemic hit.

For fourteen months, nobody came to visit. The academy is a nonprofit, so our funding comes primarily from visitors to the school. Most of our kids pay forty-five dollars a month and come from underserved populations. We have gifted kids, average kids, and kids who struggle academically.

Although we taught remotely during the pandemic, I was still trying to teach in a dynamic way. I had an ironing board set up in the shower so that I could write on the tile walls and then erase it like a whiteboard. It was a makeshift mess. It was a horrible time.

When the Great Depression hit in 1929, people told a young animator that his little movies about a cartoon mouse wouldn't do well in that grave economic climate. Walt Disney replied, "What better time is there to help make people smile?" Disney got stronger during the Great Depression instead of getting weaker. Sometimes great things are born out of sad times. Things that, if we're lucky, make our lives just a little better.

At the Ron Clark Academy (RCA), we have always been about "What's big? What's next?" But while we were rebounding from the pandemic, I just couldn't ask my staff to do all these big things. That's why, at that annual staff retreat, I said, "Let's come up with ways that we could be just a little better. And maybe if we each do ten of them, they'll have a big impact on our school."

I put the staff into teams and asked them to brainstorm. I remember that Renita Burns, our front desk receptionist, said to me, "Mr. Clark, I already do everything the way we are supposed to do it. I'm already operating at one hundred percent. I can't be no more perfect." And honestly, she did her job well. We ask the staff to answer the phones with a smile and say, "Ron Clark Academy" in a way that has a sing-songy ring to it. She already did that and remained smiling throughout the call, giving off such good energy that made a huge impact.

I suggested that instead of just saying, "Ron Clark Academy," Ms. Burns could say, "Ron Clark Academy. Good morning. This is Renita." I thought that using her first name would add a personal touch. "That's easy," Renita said. "That feels like one percent, and I can do that." I also suggested that instead of saying, "Hold, please," she should ask, "May I put you on hold, please?" Again, she said, "That's easy."

I then suggested, "Maybe when parents enter the school, instead of sitting down and asking them to sign in, perhaps you should stand up, greet them at the door, hug them, walk them over to the counter, show them where to sign in, and then take them to their seat while they wait for their child." Renita responded, "Uh. That's a lot of getting up and sitting down. That sure feels like more than one percent." I instructed her, "You're right, scratch it off the list! We are only coming up with easy one percent items on our lists." But then I suggested, "Actually, maybe you should leave it on the list but only do it once a week for a random parent." She thought for a second, and then Renita agreed, saying, "That's easy. I can do that."

The next week, she came running up to me, screaming, "Mr. Clark, Mr. Clark, I've got to do it for every parent." "Do what?" I asked, and she explained, "A parent came in, and I said, 'Whoop, this is my time to do my one time a week,' and I stood up, met the parent at the door, hugged her, walked her to the desk, and guided her to her seat, and she turned and said, 'Mrs. Burns, I love you. You just made me feel so special.'" Renita then said pointedly, "So you see, I have to do it for every parent." I smiled as I answered, "Well, if you want to."

What started as a one percent grew into something truly beautiful and changed the entire energy in our lobby, but we didn't stop there. We came up with a lot of great ideas that day—some for admin and support staff like Renita, and others for teachers and even parents. Many of them are in this book, and I hope they inspire you to come up with a few ways to be one percent better on your own. In addition, I'm including Teacher Shoutouts in sidebars so you can see how teachers all over the country have been embracing this idea of small changes making big differences. You'll also see some Super Boost tips for those days when you've got a little more time or energy, as well as a few half percent tips for those rough February Mondays when you're deprived of sunlight and tapped out. It would be wonderful if we had the time every day to support each student with their extracurriculars the way I did with Ronnie Martin at that basketball game long ago. But smaller and sometimes less individualized efforts give us big payoffs, too.

It hasn't been long, but since that staff retreat, I've seen that when you improve every aspect of your school or organization by a tiny bit, the collective improvement resonates throughout your community, creating more opportunity for improvement, growth, learning, and joy. And the best part is that they're easy changes, so you can make them even when you think you're already doing everything right—or when you feel like the well is dry.

I invite you to see the difference these small changes can make.

SEND PARENTS A QUICK PICTURE

During test taking, I used to monitor the room while thinking, "There's a thousand things I need to be doing instead of standing here and watching these kids take this test." But if a kid has a question, their teacher has to be there to answer it. So, I'd sit there, trying not to dwell on all the other work I needed to do that day.

Then one day I pulled out my phone and took a picture of a kid who looked like she was giving the test her all. I texted the picture to her mom, saying, "I don't know what grade she's going to make on this test, but she's working really hard. She's trying her best. You should be proud of her either way."

I got a quick and delighted text message back, "Thank you so much for seeing potential in my child. Thank you for believing in her!" Well, the child failed the test, but that's not the point. The mom appreciated me and realized that I saw potential in her child. It might seem like just a little photo, but to that mom it was more. That photo was a sign that I was thinking about her daughter and her mom as well.

One of the big mistakes teachers make is imagining parents as sleeping bears that we are afraid to wake up. Teachers are afraid to poke the bear, because as long as they leave them alone, they won't cause any drama in the classroom.

Typically, a teacher will say, "I have a student with a discipline problem."

The teacher takes the kid to the principal, and the principal will say, "Have you called the parent?"

"No, I haven't."

"Well, call the parent, then. Try that first."

And the teacher will think, "Lord, she is really sending me back to this class with this bad kid. Give me mercy!"

Later the teacher will call the parent, saying, "Your son is causing problems." The parent will talk to their kid, and the kid will behave better for two or three days. But when the kid begins misbehaving again, the parent won't do anything this time because of the games kids play. You see, each day their kid will go home and tell their parent, "That teacher doesn't like me. She's picking on me." Naturally, the kid's best friend will back them up and say, "Yeah, other kids talk, but that teacher always blames your son, and he doesn't do anything wrong." Suddenly, the parent thinks you're the problem, not their child.

But what if you had taken fifteen seconds to text the parent? You might say, "I just want to let you know he was so much better today. Thank you for talking to him. You're a wonderful mom."

If you had done that, when the kid tells his mom you always pick on him, his mom will tell him she has been talking to you and she's not buying his story. It might seem like a small thing, but anything that opens lines of communication, trust, and friendship is a huge deal.

TEACHER SHOUTOUT

MARILYN O'HALLORAN
CLARK COUNTY SCHOOL DISTRICT, LAS VEGAS, NV

One thing I do as a small boost is start the first day of school looking for students showing courtesy, whether it be holding the door open for others or something else—any random act of kindness I can compliment. I then take a picture of the student and send the photo to the family.

By the end of the first week, I make sure to have caught each student being kind in some way. The photo also allows for families to have something to talk about and give positive praise to their child at home. I do this periodically throughout the year, and students love it. They are so happy when I bring out the "Caught Being Kind" sign.

WELCOME POTENTIAL TEACHERS—AND SUPPORT NEW COLLEAGUES

"Some of you haven't been turning in your attendance sheets. I need those turned in daily," said Mrs. Robinson, the principal, who was looking sternly around the staff meeting.

I froze. I was one month into my first semester teaching, and I broke out in a sweat. I had never turned in an attendance sheet. Not one. No one had told me! I turned to a colleague named Barbara Jones and whispered, "I haven't turned in any attendance sheets. She's talking about me!" Barbara replied, "No, she's not. I've been turning them in for you every day."

"What?" I couldn't believe it.

"Yeah, I've been doing your attendance sheets. You shouldn't have to worry about that right now." I'd been so stressed trying to grade papers, deal with discipline issues, contact parents, and plan my lessons. I felt like I was floundering every moment.

But Barbara found a way to help. It meant the world to me.

We all need to be like Barbara Jones. And that person can be you, and it starts from the moment you hire new teachers to join your team.

When I'm interviewing someone for a teaching position, I encourage my staff to engage with and support the candidate by walking through the lobby and introducing themselves. A current teacher might say to a prospective one, "How are you doing? My name's Michael. It's nice to meet you. Are you applying to work here? We'd love to have you as part of our school. It's a great team here. Everyone works well together. Hope you can join us. It was nice to meet you."

The whole profession must do a better job of generating good publicity. Do you know what happens way too often now? There will be a teacher sitting in an office, waiting to interview for a position. A teacher who works at the school will be in the office making copies or doing something else and say, "Oh, hey! I don't think I know you. You're applying to work here? Oh, good! Girl, we need some *help*. These kids are about to kill me. Can you start today? What grade are you applying to teach? Oh, sixth grade? Hell, no. See, I taught those kids two years ago. Those kids are the ones who gave me the psoriasis."

I want everyone who applies to work at our school to walk out the door and think, "Gosh, I hope I get that job. I really want that job." I want them to go into the community and tell people that. It's good publicity.

It's a great idea to do all you can to welcome new educators and staff to your school. It's important to let them know they're appreciated and that they're part of a team. I suggest you meet with a few of your colleagues and come up with small but impactful ways you can celebrate and uplift new members of the team.

For example, you could offer to do a chore for a new teacher. Often, new teachers are given the worst bus duties and the worst lunch duties. So be generous one day! Say, "Hey, I'll cover this for you today. You don't have to worry about it." Give them a few extra moments to get their lessons ready, prepare, and catch their breath; a lot of new teachers are still figuring out time management, and they can get overwhelmed.

Offering to do a duty for a colleague is a small thing that can alleviate some stress in their life and make them feel supported. If it's someone's birthday, you could work with your colleagues to adjust the schedule so they can leave early that day. Just set it up and then tell them, "We've got your classes covered. You can leave early today." I remember when a teacher did something special like that for me. It made me feel seen and supported.

We'd just had a new person join our office staff, Leah Thompson. On her very first day at the front desk, the staff sent her a bouquet of flowers with a little note welcoming her to the team and letting her know we love her. When she saw it, she had tears in her eyes. It was a little gesture, but it went a long way. I bet she went home and told her family, "Look at the bouquet of flowers!" She probably took pictures and sent them to her parents. Small, supportive gestures like that can have a strong effect on how someone feels about their job.

Just ask Barbara Jones!

HALF PERCENT BOOST
WHAT A GOOD BOY!

One thing you can do is buy a few boxes of dog biscuits and put them in plastic bags to give to students and staff members with pets. (It's easy to learn the pets' names since people love talking about them.) Then write a note: "Dear Rex, I thought you might like this bone. I hear you've been a good boy." Sign your name, and put the note in the baggie with the dog biscuits and give the bag to the staff member or student. Tell them, "Oh, I thought Rex might like that." Kids love that stuff and being able to tell their families, "Oh, Mr. Clark sent Rex a dog bone." Staff members enjoy going home with a treat for their best friend, too.

CLIMB HIGH—
BUT DON'T FALL

Thirty years ago, I was in class and noticed some kids in the back row passing notes or something—I couldn't see what they were up to. So, I stood on a chair. As soon as I could see the back row clearly, they all froze. I thought, "I wish I were this tall all the time."

That's why I started standing on chairs. Occasionally, I would step on a desk. The desks we have at RCA are more like tables, so they're safe for me. Sometimes teachers will come to our school and say, "I don't think they're going to let me stand on my desk when I go home." I tell them that they don't have to, but it's a trick that has given me a better view of the class and imparts a certain authority. Some teachers will look defeated that they can't stand on a desk in the classroom, but you don't have to stand on a desk to be a great teacher; it's just one of many strategies you can use.

And, if you don't want to stand on a chair or a desk, loads of people have come up with variations that achieve the same result.

For example, my colleague Kim Bearden didn't want to stand on a desk because she was worried she would fall, and additionally, she often wore skirts to school. So, for safety and modesty's sake, we bought a hundred dollars' worth of plywood and built a stage at the front of her class that makes her eleven inches taller.

It turns out that a stage has a variety of in-class uses! Yes, standing center stage makes you feel confident in the command you have of the classroom, and students can see you more clearly. It can also build connections with students. Teacher Jenna Sistrunk made a stage, and every year she lets her students sign it.

"All my babies sign my stage," she told me, "and that made it even more special for me. It's something that I'm sure will become even more special in the years to come."

Students can use the stage to present to the class as well, giving them confidence in those speaking and listening skills.

Another teacher, Avery Lieske, said, "Adding a stage has helped my students tremendously. It's helped them develop more confidence."

Tracey Lynn Street didn't build a stage. Instead, she took the legs off some of her tables. "They make great stages, and I store things underneath." Very clever.

Another teacher, Alana Robillard, said, "I absolutely love my stage. Having a stage . . . helps me deliver my instruction in an engaging and powerful way. I love how I'm able to reel them in as I work the room. My students love the stage as well. The stage has also helped them build up their confidence as they work the room and teach their peers."

TEACHER SHOUTOUT

NICOLE TSCHAPPAT,
HARMONY ELEMENTARY SCHOOL, GOSHEN, KY

Having a stage has been a positive for me as a teacher. It is a visual cue for my students that I need them to track me. I am short, so it gives me visibility. I also feel more confident and ready to teach. My students love it, too! They love to be on the stage to present and share their thinking. The stage helps them make eye contact and engage the audience. I love watching their confidence grow each time they are onstage. My stage breaks into four parts so I can change it to fit the teaching scenario.

PUT SOMETHING–
ANYTHING–
ON THE BOARD

When kids enter my classroom, I want to provide a quick, focused transition into what we will be studying for the day. Having something already on the board when they get there shows that I'm ready to teach and prepares something for the kids who settle in really fast to focus on during transitional moments.

Those moments are important because you never want dead time in a classroom. So, as soon as they come in, have something on the board—nothing complicated, just a puzzle, or a math problem, or a few questions. Something to focus them while they're waiting for everyone to get ready for the lesson. I know this must seem like such an obvious thing for teachers to do, but as I traveled to all fifty states and visited over three hundred school systems, I can't tell you how many classes I saw where the students would enter and the teacher would wait for everyone to be settled before they would begin.

A leveled-up way to create a focused transition is to have some light music playing when the students come in and have five review questions from the day before written on the board. Then, call on the first student to raise their hand to answer the questions. As other students are getting their homework out and getting ready to go, that student is already trying to answer each question. Hearing a student already engaging with the teacher speeds up other students' transition time, and you can bet there'll be another student who thinks they have the right answers to your questions.

If the first student gets an answer right, they get to keep going. If they get all five right in a row, turn the music up, and everyone can cheer as they're getting into their seats. If the student gets one wrong, the next student to raise their hand gets to try and answer.

This strategy offers students a responsibility when they enter that room. There is a reason for them to get their materials out quickly; I'm intentional about that. I want to reduce chaos, speed up slow-moving students, and not waste a second of class time.

Having questions on the board also keeps a record of what's important to review. Once, a parent told me their child was having trouble knowing what to focus on when studying for an assessment. "Well," I said, "every day I put five review questions on the board. I suggest that he use his tablet to snap a quick picture of the board. After nine weeks, he'll have a ton of pictures he can use to review."

Those review questions not only help students transition into the class but also serve as effective study guides at the end of the term.

SUPER-BOOST!

A LOUD WAY TO PROMOTE SWIFT ENGAGEMENT!

Sometimes, I blow up balloons and put one on every child's desk with a magic marker. There is a math problem placed on the board, and when the students come in, they immediately start solving it on the balloon. Why are they so invested? If they get it right, they can sit on the balloon and pop it.

While this is a fun activity, it takes some effort to blow up the balloons and tie knots in them; your hands will hurt. But if you do this occasionally, your students will have a real impetus to solve math problems—plus it adds to their anticipation, never knowing if today is the day there will be balloons on the desks.

5

PLAY BINGO

"Bingo!"

The gym erupted with joy—it was as if everyone had won! Students cheered, the parents were laughing and whistling, staff members jumped up and down, and the other seniors were roaring with laughter. One of their own, a woman from the nearby senior living facility, had just won $400 at our school's Bingo Night. She raised her arms up high like a champion, and the cheers got even louder.

That's what it's all about, isn't it? It had been so easy, making a moment like that—it was just an invitation to the nearby senior living facility. "Would you like to come to Bingo Night?" There is nothing more meaningful than reaching out and making people feel special and included—it takes so little and means so much. It was beautiful.

I started doing Bingo Night with just parents at first. It was easy; you can buy fourteen hundred bingo sheets for $14.95 online. Then I asked local companies to donate fun prizes and whatnot. The fact is, people love bingo. It's a great way for shy people to socialize because they have something to do and talk about; it's also a perfect way for us to meet our students' parents and build real relationships with them. It's important to have events at school where there's no threat of talk about grades. One of my one percenters is that I place a sign on the gymnasium door that says, "There is to be no talk about discipline, grades, or academics tonight. Tonight's just bingo."

Once I had set up Bingo Night, I began making little additions. I would push around a cart with a big bowl filled with apples, Snickers, and Sprites. I would go up to each table and ask the parents if anyone wanted a snack. "Can I get you anything?"

Then one of our staff members, Paula Williams, realized I should be inviting the seniors at the senior living facility to the event. Why hadn't I thought of it sooner? We have been sharing events with local seniors since 2008, when our students sang Christmas carols for them before Christmas break. One day I had left RCA, and when I looked over at the senior facility, it looked so somber and alone. I drove over to the office and asked if it would be possible to bring some students over the next day to sing Christmas carols for the seniors.

"Yes, we would love it! Right after lunch would be great because everyone would be around." So the next day after lunch, we took the students across the street to the facility, and we sang Christmas carols. We still have pictures up from the event because the students were so joyful. The seniors were clapping, laughing, cheering, and hugging the kids. They even began singing with them. All we had to do was walk across the street, sing for them, and walk back.

So, when Paula Williams said she wanted to invite the seniors to bingo, I was all in! We even arranged for a limo from a local rental company to pick up the seniors in style and deliver them to the school. Once they arrived, they had a red carpet to walk on and a special VIP table set up with snacks right at the front of the bingo room.

It wasn't until that joyous reaction to the big four-hundred-dollar prize that I realized we had built something community-wide. What started out as a simple way to connect to parents grew into a multi-generational event that sparks joy. To me, Bingo Night is an example of something that starts out as a small effort but organically grows into something meaningful that can define your school and your students' educational experience.

6

BUTTON UP

I tried not to show it on my face, but our parent committee read my skepticism loud and clear. I didn't think it would work.

They had just informed me that they had a great one percent to add to their list. They said it would be a *great* way to make sure our staff could recognize which student belonged to which parent. "We'll use a button machine to make buttons with the name and picture of each kid and the name of their parent. We'll give these buttons to the parents and ask them to wear them whenever they come to the school."

I thought there was no way the parents would wear the buttons. They'd accept them, sure—but then they'd leave them in their car, forget them at home, or simply put them in a drawer and never think about them again.

The committee tried to convince me. "We'll affirm them every time we see parents with the button and say, 'Thank you so much for wearing the button.'"

"Yeah," I replied, "but I don't think they'll wear the buttons in the first place."

They stood firm. "Well, can we try it?" This was during our one percent improvement brainstorm, so I didn't feel as if I should say no.

Instead, I said, "It feels like more than one percent effort, but if you want to, give it a shot."

"It'll be easy! We can use our button machine and knock it right out."

I still had my doubts, and I honestly felt bad saying yes because I knew it wouldn't work.

About a month later, I saw a mom leaving after our Bingo Night and couldn't quite place her. I visit the homes of every kid I teach (a thirty percent effort), but I realized that this mother had probably been wearing a face mask during my visit. That night, I called out to her, "Bye, Mom! And thanks for coming to Bingo Night." Then she turned. I saw that button, and I knew who it was!

I walked over and said, "Oh, my gosh. Can I tell you something? Your son is working so hard. He's doing such a great job. He's really turned it around. You should be really proud of him."

Her whole face lit up. "Mr. Clark, my family's had a lot of bad news lately, and I needed some good news. Thank you so much." She hugged me real tight and then walked off.

I just thought, "Damn, it was that *button*." If it hadn't been for that button, I wouldn't have known who that mom was, and I wouldn't have been able to make that connection and give a little lift to that family going through a tough time.

Sometimes it's great to be wrong about something. The buttons worked tremendously! On our end-of-the-year survey, the parents ranked the buttons as their favorite new addition to RCA! We took their kids to KENYA, and yet the buttons ranked higher. I highly recommend your school try it; it's a winner.

APPEAL TO THE SENSES

What's the most immediate way to create a more welcoming space? Appeal directly to the five senses and focus on what your students smell or hear or see or feel or taste. It can be an easy, straightforward, and stress-free way to improve the climate and culture of your classroom.

Our senses are not called into service in the classroom often enough, and yet they are important tools we are given as human beings to assess, understand, judge, communicate, and enjoy. Try using a few of these tips to build a more engaging classroom experience.

LEARN 'N SNIFF

I put a plug-in air freshener in my room because I want my eighth graders to walk in and say, "I like this classroom. It smells good in here." A good scent is an easy way to let students know they are someplace pleasant and safe. Remember when we were kids? We'd get a scratch 'n sniff sticker and be so excited to scratch and sniff it. If a student acts like they're not excited to get these stickers, they're lying. They're going to scratch and smell it and love it. Occasionally giving out a fruity-smelling treat like this can be just the thing you need to up the interest and excitement in your class by one percent.

SUPER-BOOST!

MOVIE AND POPCORN

One year, we had our students make short films that dealt with suspense. We showed them how to build the climax, add music, and do short, quick scenes that really added to the anticipation of the moment. Then once all the students had made their short films, we showcased them in our auditorium. As the students walked in, there was a special surprise. A local movie theater had donated a popcorn machine to us, so we made popcorn for the whole school. It smelled delicious! As the students walked in, they were so excited to get their bag of popcorn, and as they sat down, they snuggled into their seats and dipped their hands into their popcorn bags. You could see the glee and anticipation on their faces. The popcorn made it. The smell added to the atmosphere and made the moment just perfect.

SOUNDING GOOD

Sound can motivate, energize, and reward your students, or simply help you educate them. For motivation and to start class efficiently, I like to have music playing each day when students enter and exit my classroom. When music is playing, they walk faster, get their items ready quicker, and don't talk. When I don't play music, they move slower, drag their feet, and take forever to find their materials. I also want students to feel great as they enter my classroom, so I stand at the door and speak to every kid as they come in. That way, they feel seen and important to me.

To add some energy and fun to the class—or if you want to reward a hardworking class with a treat—you can go online and record yourself speaking to the students, then use AI and have that message altered so it sounds like the students' favorite actor or NBA player. You can even have the president give them a message. Then, in the middle of class, you can tell the kids, "You have done so well. I have a special treat for you." When you press play, your message will sound like LeBron James or the president of the United States. Your students will freak out!

Another thing you can do involving sound to make teaching easier and less tiring for you is to wear a microphone that amplifies your voice. A company called Audio Enhancement developed the most amazing microphone for teachers, and it has changed my life. I love to make big sounds and do fun voices as I'm teaching, but it can be straining on my voice. However, with the enhancement I can talk in a regular voice. I never have to raise my voice; it is amplified so every student hears every bit of the lesson clearly. They hear what I'm saying, and I don't have to strain my voice all day. After wearing the microphone for a week, I realized that when I went home I was less tired and had more energy; because I wasn't straining my voice all day, my body was less stressed. The microphone was definitely a blessing for all of my students, because they could all hear me clearly, but it ended up being a tremendous lifesaver for me as well.

DRUMMING UP SUPPORT THROUGH TOUCH

Even I thought I might be crazy to ask students to bang drums in the classroom. Turns out, I wasn't—at least not for that. Drumming really can support student engagement and help struggling students stay focused!

All you need are some empty paint buckets from a home improvement store. When I first started out with drumming in the classroom, I gave paint buckets to those students who needed help focusing and told them to place them under their desks and play them whenever their classmates were clapping for each other or if a drum roll was appropriate. If I made a joke, I'd expect to hear *ba-dum-bum*. As a result, the students who had the paint buckets became really focused on the lesson. That was huge, especially since they were the students who had trouble paying attention. After a while, we invested in djembes. Now, the students hold the drum for the whole class and pay attention and focus for the entire lesson because they need to be ready to tap the drum at any moment. Teaching active listening skills can be tough with some kids, but this method made them *want* to be attentive.

Another way to use touch to increase engagement and peer support is to ask students to use their hands in class to share their opinions. For example, if I say something in class that students really agree with, they will raise their hands with their pinky and thumb out and three middle fingers down—kind of like bull horns—and shake them at me. That shows that they like what I'm saying or agree with me. If a student is making comments and other students agree with them, they are encouraged to turn and do the horns toward that student, essentially saying, "I agree with you."

I see the real power in this simple, fun exercise. When I travel around the country watching educators teach, it's clear that we have a lot of students struggling to focus. There might be one student answering a teacher's question while the rest of the class spaces out. Or maybe a few of them will have their hands up and waving at the teacher—but these students are so anxious to speak that they aren't paying any attention to the other child. So, by letting students raise up their horns and shake them at each other, you allow students to become and stay involved.

I agree

When my students hold both of their hands flat and start shaking them, that says that they think the speaker is on the wrong track. As you might imagine, the students really, really like that. I also like it, because it starts conversations in class. And finally, if students extend their arms toward a student and wave their fingers, that indicates they're giving that student energy and support. These gestures have added a lot to our class.

I disagree

Sometimes, though, the day is long, and students just lose engagement. Once, when this happened, I took a trash can in my class and put it on the right side of the room in front of the board. I put another trash can at the left side and told my students that, every few minutes or so, I was going to pick which side of the class was most engaged. When I named the most focused side, all of those students then got to ball up a sheet of paper and shoot it at the trash can on their side of the room. Every student that made a shot got one point. You'd have thought I took the kids to an NBA game. They all woke up. But then the students in the back row said, "This isn't fair; we're so far away." "Good point. Why don't you write a three on your sheets of paper because you're shooting for three-pointers?" They loved that. At the end of the class, the kids were laughing and joking. I was thrilled because I got them to pay attention to everything I had said.

It's funny how the sense of touch and the little gestures we associate with play or with communication can add so much to learning and to your school culture. The students walked out of class saying, "That was so fun," and isn't that the point? The lesson, honestly, was dry material, but the trash-baskets made the whole experience a slam dunk.

THE TASTE OF SUCCESS

If you want to do something as an administrator to really get your staff excited to use their sense of taste, get the cafeteria team to bake you some homemade cookies, put them on the tray, and walk through the school, bringing a fresh-baked cookie to each staff member. These smell and taste delicious, adding a highlight to the day.

Every day at lunch, I tutor a few students who want to improve their math, using worksheets with five or six math questions. One day, the last math question was a word problem dealing with how many cookies you would have to sell to reach a desired total. One of the students, Aubrey Land, said, "I would love some of those cookies right now."

"Well, you know what?" I replied. "Maybe we should order some on Uber Eats."

Right away the kids asked, "Really? Really?"

"If we order them now, they won't arrive before lunch is over," I said, "but they will be here for snack at the end of the day, and we can have them then." The students were even more excited when I pulled out my phone and said, "But first, let's determine how much money it's going to cost to get each one of us one of these cookies." We had to figure out different prices, taxes, delivery charge fees, and tip costs. The whole thing became a math lesson.

At the end of the day, these students came running up to me asking, "Mr. Clark, Mr. Clark, did you really get the cookies?"

"Of course I did." I pulled the cookies out from the kitchen, and the students began jumping up and down, hugging each other. It was just cookies, but the students were so thrilled. The important thing to remember is they weren't excited because they were going to get a cookie; they were excited because it was unexpected. When you do a little something the students don't expect, it has an impact. And that's something that great teachers do.

You probably won't be surprised to read that the next day at lunch I had thirty students clamoring around me to get the tutoring worksheet.

"Don't expect me to order cookies every day," I said.

"Oh, we don't, Mr. Clark," they replied innocently.

I knew they secretly did, so I told them that had been a special surprise for a group of kids who had worked hard yesterday. I looked at Aubrey Land, and she was grinning from ear to ear.

PLAY A GROSS, FUN FOOD GAME!

You can add fun to your classroom by buying a Harry Potter–themed box of assorted-flavor jelly beans. As you may or may not know, a lot of them are delicious. Some taste like watermelon, and others taste like strawberry—but some of them are absolutely disgusting. There are vomit-flavored beans, earwax-flavored ones, and even worse ones, if you can imagine.

In class, tell your students that you'll be having a competition. You'll review content with them like a quiz, and whichever side of the room gets a question right gets to pick a student from the other side who has to eat a jelly bean. They might get a great one—or one that's not so great. If *both* sides get it right at the same time, then the teacher must eat the bean. This makes students want to try hard so the teacher is trapped into eating a horrible bean.

It's something silly and fun, but I've learned time and again over thirty years of teaching that taking a little bit of effort to do something different goes a long way in the eyes of students.

SEEING IT

By putting personal, perhaps unexpected things up in the classroom, I try my best to show my students who I am. How can we expect to

32

connect with students if they don't know who we are, what we like, and where we come from?

I'll put up a photo of me with my Chow Chows. I know seeing those pictures of my dogs licking my face will resonate with the dog lovers in the room. Perhaps there are some of you reading this right now who instantly like me better because I am a dog person.

It's also fascinating for students to see photos of me when I was their age. They really connect with that kid, particularly when I tell them about my old insecurities, my fears, and the names I was afraid other students would call me. When you show your students who you are and let them see your vulnerabilities, they'll like you more and be more likely to bond with you.

A fun way to add visual interest to your classroom is to put students' faces on worksheets. Years ago, one of my students did not want to do my homework, but he loved football. So I cut a picture of his favorite football player out of a magazine, cut his face out of the yearbook, placed the footballer's picture on top, and copied it on the worksheets. It looked realistic! The student loved it, and he did the worksheet. Now, thanks to AI and online editing tools, you don't have to use scissors and glue. You can just go into an editing program and crop out the student's face, place it where you want, and add it to the worksheet. It brings it to life. Doing this personalizes learning for kids in an increasingly data-driven learning culture.

Another way of using images to have fun is a game I play using an app called Viggle.AI. You can take a picture of your school's principal and make the person dance, jump up and down, or do whatever you want. At the beginning of class, tell students, "If you pay attention, at the end of class we're going to press this button, and we'll make the principal dance." As you might imagine, the students want to see that! (However, I'd recommend that you get the permission of the principal ahead of time, so they don't randomly learn you made them dance in your classroom.)

GUESS THE MASKED TEACHER

To build a school culture that is fully inclusive, you must build fun experiences for students and staff to have together. Otherwise, your culture might become too boring and hierarchical, with students thinking that the teachers are on the opposing team. It doesn't cost a lot of money or time to build these fun shared experiences; all it takes is a little thought about how to lighten everyone's day.

One of the ways we do it is by occasionally having a Masked Teacher perform for our students. During lunchtime, our cafeteria team brings out a bedsheet, carefully holding it up like a screen. When they lower the bedsheet slightly, a staff member is standing there, wearing a Halloween mask, but only the mask is visible. Then the staff member sings thirty seconds of a song. When time is up, a staff member asks the kids, "Anyone know who that is? Who do you think is behind the mask?"

The kids go wild guessing. "It's Mr. Brown!" "No, it's Mr. Bernadin!" It's a quick and fun break in the day that creates a shared moment of laughter between staff, teachers, and students. Believe me, students see that teacher in a whole new—and fun!—light.

When the singer takes off the mask, whether the students were wrong or right, they start laughing and applauding. Everyone loves a masked singer!

And it's easy to do. All you need is a blanket or a sheet and a mask. Ask two staff members to hold up the blanket—and make sure they block the students' view of the singer as they enter the cafeteria. The singer is crouching behind the sheet. When they pull down the sheet a little bit, the masked staff member stands up straight, revealing only their head. Then they sing for thirty seconds.

Another way for students to have relaxed fun with the staff is to play Last Person Standing. This is a school-wide game where only a single winner is left standing at the end. The great thing is that this game has loads of action but only takes about ten minutes at the end of the school day.

I ask the entire student body and staff to head to the gym at the end of school. Then I instruct everyone to pick one of the four corners of the gym and go stand in it. I have numbered each corner of the gym. Now, I hold up four sheets of paper, numbered 1 through 4.

"I'm going to close my eyes and shuffle these sheets of paper and then raise one in the air. If I raise your number in the air, your group is out. You must come sit in the center of the gym floor." I shuffle the pages and then raise one of them, and everyone from the selected corner has to go to the center and sit down. Next, I play music and tell everyone to select a new corner as the music's playing. The staff members and students start running around switching corners until the music stops. More and more people are knocked out until, at the end of Last Person Standing, only one person is left.

It's just something quick to do in the last ten minutes of the school day, but the students love seeing the staff running around enjoying the suspense just as much as they do. And when students leave for home, they are smiling, excited, jumping up and down. This costs even less than the Masked Teacher, and it's just as short. But the aftereffects of the student-teacher bonds last for a long time. Both games are great ways to create moments where the students are wondering, "When is it going to happen again? Are they going to do this more often?"

SUPER-BOOST!

MAKE YOUR OWN MAGIC COMMITTEE!

Speaking of magic, we have a Magic Committee at our school. Starting a Magic Committee is a ten percent tip that consists of asking people to create a bunch of one percent tips. Everybody wants to be on the Magic Committee because it involves doing fun things throughout the school year for the entire school. For example, on Pi Day (March 14), the Magic Committee had a pie-eating contest in which representatives from each class tied their hands behind their backs, bent over, and tried to eat an entire pie. The pies were small—just four inches—but it was so exciting and something fun to break up the day.

The Magic Committee has also done karaoke during lunchtime. Another time, at the end of the day, all the students went out to the courtyard to have a Hula-Hoop competition. Earlier that day, the students had done a Hula-Hoop competition in PE to determine the grade winners. Those winners then advanced to the school-wide competition in the courtyard, and everyone was laughing and joking and cheering. Everyone had fun. Another day, the Magic Committee let all the students out of school ten minutes early, and there were flavored slushies in the courtyard for everyone. The students were smiling, jumping up and down, and celebrating. It was like summer came early, and nothing is more magical than that!

PASS OUT CARPOOL POPS

Sometimes it seems like the best signs of appreciation are the unexpected ones. What I like to do is create a sense of anticipation—just like with those freshly baked cookies in chapter 7. A treat out of the blue every now and then lightens everyone's day.

Students aren't the only ones who should have anticipation built into their days—far from it. Parents are rushing through traffic from work to pick up their kids before heading home to get dinner together and do the dishes and their chores. So seeing a smiling face and receiving a warm greeting and a cool popsicle can create a surprising, refreshing oasis in the day. About once a month, our team hands out ice pops to the parents in the carpool line. They have music playing outside, and as they hand the treats out, they tell the parents, "We appreciate you."

Just like on Bingo Night, you're building real relationships anytime you make an effort to let them know they are valued.

TEACHER SHOUTOUT

BRANDIE MITCHELL,
LIBERTY ELEMENTARY, SIOUX CITY, IA

We wanted to find more ways to include and honor our students' parents. It's just one small act, but on the last day of school, we greeted parents curbside with a choice of coffee or lemonade. Their reactions were the best—I wish we had been recording! Parents were surprised and grateful, and it definitely brought a smile to their faces. So simple, yet so successful in many ways.

10

SHARE
THE PRAISE

Sometimes, changing the conversation can really improve your connection with hard-to-reach students. Too often, they're defensive and either expecting criticism or to be ignored and treated like a lost cause.

Sometimes, when I have a student who I believe thinks this way, I grab a staff member and say, "Mr. Brown, when you see this kid, can you go up to him and say, 'Oh, Mr. Clark was talking about you yesterday.' And when the kid asks, 'About what?' tell him, 'Yeah, he was telling everybody at the staff meeting how much potential he thinks you have. He thinks you really could be a great student. And if you work a little bit harder, you could do extremely well in his class.'"

The next time the kid comes into my class, I'll say something like, "Hey, buddy, can we have a good day today?"

It never fails. He'll always say, "Yes, sir."

Even though the afterglow of this praise only seems to amend negative behavior for two or three days, it's still important to build these glimmers of self-confidence.

It's also important to be open to letting things happen organically. My colleague Kim Bearden once told me a powerful example of sharing praise with a student in an unexpected way. There was a student in her class with a discipline problem, and Kim was struggling to build a deeper relationship with him to help curb the behavior issues. After a poetry class, the student said, "Mrs. Bearden, you're really good at writing these poems!"

This gave Kim an idea. That night she wrote a poem for the student about the talents she saw in him. She gave him the poem the next day and said, "I wanted you to have this."

"What is it?"

"You said you like the way I write poems. So, I wrote a poem to let you know all the talents and the potential I see in you."

"Would you read it for me?"

"Sure." Kim read him the poem.

The student couldn't believe it. He asked, "How did you know? How did you know all these things about me?"

"Well, I see you. I see you in my class, and I recognize all your potential."

He asked Kim to read the poem to the whole class, which surprised her, but she was happy to do so. That night, the boy's mother called Kim and said, "You've completely changed my child. He ran home with this poem in his hand and said, 'You're not going to believe what happened. The most amazing thing happened to me at school today.'"

It took Kim a few minutes to write a simple poem to give a student belief in his potential and abilities, but it changed that child's life, not just for the school year, but possibly forever. A piece of paper changed the conversation.

TEACHER SHOUTOUT

ERICA BLACK-VEAL
CHARLOTTE-MECKLENBURG SCHOOLS, CHARLOTTE, NC

Watch a new or veteran teacher secretly for a few days. One day, interrupt their class and explain to the students that their teacher is always bragging about them. Call out one or two students who misbehave to note that they are hard workers and try so hard. Or call out two students who don't get a lot of recognition. Tell them how you have noticed a change in their maturity and work ethic. Works every time.

FACE THE CLASS

When you teach, there is a simple thing you can do with your body to make the lesson run more smoothly, show your students you are happy to be in the room with them, and keep steady control of the classroom: write on the board while facing the class.

Teachers too often write on the board with their backs to the class. That's a guaranteed way to break the flow of any classroom dialogue you've created, as well as put potential discipline problems in your blind spot. I write facing the class so I can look at everybody. That way, I never lose focus on the students or control of the classroom.

When my team went around the country observing classrooms, we consistently saw teachers writing on the board with their backs to the room. My rule is: your feet must remain facing the kids. When you break eye contact with the students, that's when they take a moment to daydream and start thinking about other things. They'll take a moment to giggle at a classmate, pass a note, or make a face behind your back.

You want to avoid that by making sure you face the students. So, take your right arm (if you're right-handed), stretch it out to your side, turn your hand toward the board, and write in that manner. Your feet are always facing the class. I'll be honest: it's going to feel awkward and backward the first time you do it. In fact, it'll probably take a week, but after a while, you'll be doing it with ease, and you won't even think about it anymore.

That way, they can see your face and recognize that you're happy and excited to be teaching them. Kids learn more easily from happy people. And happy people look at who they're talking to.

DON'T ANSWER— EXPLORE

When a kid asks a question, sometimes I don't answer it.

I just stand there and tell the classroom, "I think one of you should answer that question." For example, a kid may say something like, "Why do you think Bashar al-Assad would've done that?" I won't answer. I'll look around the class, waiting for someone to give their input. Soon, another kid will say, "Well, maybe because he was trying to retaliate." And a whole conversation starts, showing students they can offer insights about newsworthy, historical, or fictional characters. I want the students to realize I'm not the only one in the room with an opinion, and rarely am I the only one in the room with an answer worth sharing.

It's important that kids learn they have the autonomy to answer questions, even big ones. They don't need us to answer them all. We're not going to be interviewing with them or taking their SAT exams or presenting for them at work. We need to get kids over any nervousness about speaking in class or expressing opinions. (But remember, you have to create a kind classroom culture where bullying is not allowed.)

When you *do* ask questions, however, you want to ask questions that ask for even more depth of thought, questions like why and how.

You don't want to ask what. You need to ask questions that make them have to take a beat and truly think before answering.

Once again, be specific with your students about what you expect from them. It takes a while to get students used to this type of class-room. In class discussions, you might have to model some things for them at first, because students may not have learned to talk and share their ideas. When I first asked my students to speak up, they had no idea what I meant and had never seen what I wanted them to do.

So, I role-played with them. I asked them, "Does anyone know where we should start with this equation?" No one said anything, so I ran over to the side of the class and pretended I was standing up as a student. I said, "Well, Mr. Clark, I think we should start in the order of operations. The order of operations says, 'Always begin in the parentheses.' Does anyone else agree or disagree with me?" The students did not respond at all. They just sat there staring. So, I ran to the other side of the classroom and acted like *another* student, saying, "Well, I agree with Ron, and let me tell you why."

I had to do this for an entire day of asking questions, giving exam-ples of how to respond, showing them what I meant. I was playing all the roles in the classroom: the great student, the engaged student, the student who asks deep questions, the student who tries to involve other students. It was exhausting. But soon, the students started saying, "Oh, we get what you mean now." And they started answering ques-tions, turning to talk to each other, saying things like, "I appreciate that answer, but I disagree with you. Let me tell you why," or "I respectfully disagree. I don't feel like that man was an evil dictator. I feel like he was just trying to do what he had to do in the moment." Whatever you want students to do, you model it first. Once you've modeled it, you can expect the results to be better.

I like the idea of having students turn and talk to each other because in American classrooms we have something I call "invisibility cloaks."

Too many students have learned that if they don't want to participate in class, they can just shrug and the teacher will call on someone else.

So, I encourage the students to turn to each other to talk, question, and discuss the content. I encourage them to also call on other students and ask them if they have an opinion on what's been said. "Do you agree with me or disagree with me? Sarah, what would you do in this situation?" I discovered that if I call on students, they'll easily say, "I'm not sure." But when another peer calls on them, students are more inclined to give an answer. If I do call on a student and they don't know the answer, I never say, "Oh, maybe someone else can help." I dig in and make sure students know that I will not let them be invisible or silent in my class.

If I ask a question and Jermaine says, "I don't know," I will not let him off the hook. We need to engage students and encourage participation. I look at the entire class and say, "Class, we're going to handle this together." Then I start to break it down, step by step. But I keep talking to that first student. I say, "Oh, do you understand now? What can you tell me that you understand now from what I've just said? Do you know what we might do next?" And I walk through the problem. The one thing I would never do is let that child off the hook. Because if students realize, "Oh gosh, if this man calls on me, I'm going to have to pay attention and work with him until I get the answer," they will focus more in class.

And once they're focused, they'll join the dialogue. Try it!

MOVE WITH PURPOSE

13

Many teachers stand in a manner I call "chained to the board," where they rarely ever move more than a few feet from the center of the board at the front of the room. Sometimes, it can be really helpful to make sure that as you teach, your arms extend a bit over the desks on the front row. You almost want it to seem as if you are merging into the class and not separated from the students and perched at the front of the room.

I sometimes go to schools and watch educators who've heard me say that movement is important. Occasionally, they'll teach while moving around *all* the time. They'll say, "Oh the molecule weight is important. It's carbon monoxide, valence of two . . ." All of that while they dash around the room. Later, I'll sit down with them and say, "Lord have mercy, you're like a tornado. You were all over the place."

"Well," they respond, "I know you think that movement is important."

"Yeah, but you only move when the content is superfluous. You find the opportunity to move." As a teacher, you don't want to stand in the same spot the whole time, but when you move, it must be purposeful. You must stop moving when you are about to say something that's important.

To give you an example, I'd probably stand completely still to say something like this: "Patrick Henry realized that he must make a speech that would spark the people in the room to make a decision. He wanted to move them to realize that fighting for independence was the only answer."

Now I'd start to walk as I asked, "But what was Patrick Henry going to say? What words could he find that would encapsulate the emotion that he was feeling in that moment?" I'd stand still as I hit the most important content: "What he said was, 'Is life so dear, or peace so sweet, as to be purchased at the price of chains and slavery? Forbid it, Almighty God! I know not what course others may take; but as for me, give me liberty or give me death!'"

This might seem a bit tricky at first, but you'll get the hang of it. Just remember to stay still for the most important information and move when you're setting the information up.

Moving while you teach—and standing still to let the most important information have impact—livens up your classroom, keeps the students alert and thinking, and helps you stay focused as well. So, unchain yourself from that board and start roaming!

14

BAKE IT, DON'T FAKE IT

Baking for kids goes a long way. There's just something special about the kids knowing that you baked for them. It's an easy thing to do. However, this means that you really cannot go to the Publix or to the Piggly Wiggly and buy some cookies. You have to actually bake them yourself. You must take genuine home-baked items to the kids to be able to say, "I was thinking about you all last night. I'm glad I have the opportunity to teach y'all, so I baked you some cookies."

Those cookies hit different. I'll see kids take a bite of the cookie, and they'll say, "I want to save the rest for later." It really means something. It's a simple way of showing that you're willing to go above and beyond.

But if you really want to do this in a one percent way, just buy some store-bought cookies and put tinfoil over them. I ain't mad at that.

I encourage you to do this in the first month of the year, and only do it once or twice. Honestly, I can't be a Betty Crocker all year long. But baking once at the beginning of the year and then again in February is a great idea. That's when no one wants to be at school; everyone's sick of the short, dark days—so that's a good time to show the students that their teacher still cares about them. They will think, "Maybe nobody else's teacher brought them a treat like this today, but ours sure did." It makes them feel good, knowing that you thought about them outside of the classroom and you wanted to make a special effort.

I know in today's world we have many types of allergies and dietary restrictions to account for. So, if you are worried about that, at the beginning of the year you can send the parents a letter asking them to fill out a survey letting you know of any allergies or dietary restrictions you need to keep in mind when baking for the students. But if you'd rather not, just pop some non-buttered and unsalted popcorn, place it in Ziplock bags, and pass those out to your class one morning. And tell the students, "Last night I was thinking about you while I was having some popcorn and watching a movie, and I thought, 'Oh my gosh, this popcorn is so good. I wish I could share it with everybody.' So, I popped y'all popcorn, too."

TEACHER SHOUTOUT

DAWN HARTMAN
WOODLANDS MIDDLE SCHOOL, WEST PALM BEACH, FL

My tip for a small pick-me-up is giving teachers a little treat. After coming back from winter break, I gave every teacher a bag of popcorn and a handwritten card that said, "Just popped by to say have a great year." The response was crazy. Teachers who never speak to me came and thanked me and said what a nice surprise it was.

15

DON'T MEMORIZE— CHANT

Here is another way to use sounds, one that students enjoy and teachers appreciate because it genuinely helps with memorization. It also adds character to your class culture. What is it? A simple chant. Way back in 1984, I watched an episode of the TV show *Cheers* in which a bartender was helping another bartender study for a test. It was season 3, episode 16. He chanted, "Albania, Albania, you border on the Adriatic." Since then, I have always remembered that Albania borders the Adriatic Sea. A musical chant can stick in your brain for a long time.

The first peer-support chant I ever did came from the song "Wipe Me Down," and the students loved it. If someone did or said something great, I'd ask the class, "Is James on?" and the class would respond, "Wipe him down!" We'd make a motion with our hands like a wave in the direction of the child we were saluting.

I began thinking this might be a great way to get our kids to celebrate each other, get their blood flowing, wake their brains up, and engage them during the lesson. So now we have a lot of these chants. For example, if someone's doing something great, you can say something like, "To Brad," and point to Brad. Then all the students chant, "Get, get, get it." It's so simple and shows students how to boost each other up!

It's a good idea to ask students to help you create some of these chants—if *you* create it and the chant isn't cool, the chant won't stick. So, ask some of the creative students if they can help you come up with a peer-support chant they like.

But just as with the Albania chant, there's a lot of power in using chants to support tier-one skills in academic content. For example, I'll have the students sing this to memorize the order of operations:

> When we begin, we begin together.
> Parentheses first, now please be clever.
> Exponents come right next in line.
> Then we multiply and divide at the same time.
> Now, subtraction and addition
> walk it out with computation.
> It's the order of operations.
> It's the order of operations, -ations, -ations, eh, eh.

You'll recognize that this chant goes to the tune of Rihanna's song "Umbrella," and students absolutely cannot forget it. I also ask students to use hand gestures when chanting sometimes. When trying to add two negatives, the students will chant, "When you have two negatives, you will get a bigger negative," while using their hands to make a negative sign. Later, I'll watch students taking their tests, and I'll see their hands at their desks doing the little movements we do when we chant those songs. Then I know that the chant—and the physical memory—made an impact on them. Students will remember these math facts forever (just as I will never forget that Albania borders the Adriatic), but even more importantly, they'll remember the fun we had learning chants in the classroom.

16

LOOK THEM
IN THE EYES

"Students, raise your hand if I looked you in the eyes today." I tell my students to do this so I can make sure I'm connecting with them.

Too many teachers look at a class collectively and don't use eye contact to encourage dialogue. I also ask for this feedback to learn which areas I favor in the classroom. I often favor the right-hand side of my class, so I've realized I need to consciously tell myself to look left. It's very helpful to get that input about your habits.

I believe you should make sure, in every one of your classes, that you are holding each student's gaze for two seconds. This means looking into their eyes. And yes, it might feel awkward when you first start doing it, but every kid should get at least two to three seconds of straight eye contact during every lesson.

Eye contact also supports maintaining and gauging the speed of the lesson. Lessons should move at a good clip—and kids' eyes will tell you if they're bored or confused. You must keep the dialogue and the information flowing. We're dealing with a TikTok generation that will mentally swipe right if they're getting bored. You want the lesson to go fast, to be varied, and to be challenging. It can't be slow, and it can't be dull.

As you know, I want lively dialogue in my classroom. I tell students, "If you want to say something, just say it. Just speak out and say, 'Mr. Clark, did you use the Pythagorean theorem there?' or 'Mr. Clark, why do you think Henry VIII did that?'" To keep control of a classroom like that, using eye contact helps to focus the room when students start speaking out whenever they want. When two kids speak at the same time, whichever kid I happen to glance at is who gets the floor—and the other one will know to hold on for a moment.

This is when I make sure my students are learning how to use eye contact, too. Once I'm looking at that student, and that kid knows they have the floor, they stand, turn, and address the whole class as they talk. So, they'll turn to face their classmates and say, "I think you should start in the parentheses because the order of operations . . ."

I used to tell the students to turn around, and they'd just turn their shoulders toward their classmates. But now I say, "Feet," because if they turn their feet toward their classmates, their entire body follows suit. Just as a teacher's feet should always face the class, a student's feet should face their peers when they are talking, and they should use eye contact.

But as you know, some of these kids can be shy. They avoid eye contact and avoid speaking in class. To counteract this, I play a game. This game helps the shy kids get used to standing up, facing the class, and looking them in the eyes.

I have all the kids stand up, and I'll say, "Everyone, in the next twenty seconds, I'm going to try and look each one of you in the eyes. You must stare at me. If I look you in the eyes, you must sit down because I knocked you out."

I have a student act as the timer, and I go through and look at my students in the eyes. After twenty seconds, the timer will say, "All right, time." But I always make sure I don't get everybody, and I act disappointed in myself. "I missed some of you in the corners there. But hey, do any of you think you could do a better job than me?" All the kids want to play, so they come up one at a time and try to knock everyone in the class out.

Later, when these shy kids have something to say in a lesson, they feel comfortable standing up and talking. Sometimes I'll still have to say, "Feet," so they'll turn around and face the class, but now they've done this before so it's less scary. And if they aren't looking in the eyes of their peers, I will say, "Knock out," and quickly they revert to the game and start looking them all in the eyes.

Being conscious of making and maintaining eye contact does take a little effort, but you'll soon realize that this tip turns the classroom into a collaboration.

POINT
IT OUT

"Mr. Clark, what about that country right there?"

"Which one?"

"That one, under the other one." The student points at a map with their finger.

"Um, this one?"

"No. That one, shaped like a bean."

The whole class either laughs or is completely confused—or both.

This kind of confusion can waste a lot of precious teaching time.

When I had finally had enough, I bought a bunch of laser pointers and let the students use them during class time to clarify questions. Now when a kid is asking a question about a map projected on the classroom board, they can just use the laser. In math class they might say, "Mr. Clark, where'd that four come from?" The laser gives them the ability to touch the board, even from their seat, and it avoids us having to spend time playing "Which one?"

If you do want to try to use laser pointers in your classroom, I'll give you one word of advice: You will probably have students who try to make a laser light show on the ceiling or shine the laser in another student's eyes, which can be dangerous. I tell my students that if they misuse the laser pointer, they lose it. They get one opportunity and one strike. If they misuse the laser, they cannot use it for the rest of the year in my classroom. You may have to make an example of one student, but after that, the rest will realize that they shouldn't abuse the lasers or they'll lose them as well. Point made.

Make sure you research and find lasers that wouldn't do any damage if they were aimed in another student's eyes. None of us have time to deal with the drama that would bring.

JUST COME ON UP

I tell my students to just come on up to the board anytime they want to show me something or explain something. They don't really believe that I want them to do this until I add, "Nothing makes me happier than when you jump up and head to the board." It turns out that kids love standing up at the board and taking command of the class.

"Mr. Clark, everybody, do you see this right here?"

"Where did you get this five from?"

"What about this? Could we have done this problem this way?"

But if students are going to stand in the teacher's spot, I make them follow my procedure: feet to the class, make eye contact, move your hand out. In other words, they're using the same behaviors I taught them.

If the students don't see the point in learning how to address the whole class, I say, "Some of you will become teachers, but most of you won't. However, you might be the captain of a team, a CEO, a politician, a community leader, or a business owner. And you're going to need to have these skills." This makes sense to them, and they realize they're learning a real-life skill.

Sometimes you may have a situation where two students try to go up to the board at the same time; whichever child moved first gets to stand at the board. The other student must remain seated. While the child is at the front of the classroom, it's important to remind them to turn and say to the other student before they sit down, "But did you have something else that you wanted to share?" Again, this keeps the dialogue flowing.

When you have a student at the front of the classroom instructing others, leading the dialogue, it's wonderful. Sometimes I'll have students who want to come to the front of the classroom, but once they get up there, they get shy or big-eyed or lost. I tell them, "If you come up to the front of the room and forget where you are or what question you're supposed to be talking about, just say, 'I know the answer to this problem, but I'm curious if you know the answer. What do you think we should do next?'" I tell them then to call on another student for support; doing so can get them back on track.

As you might expect, you have to keep in mind that you don't want to let students go astray at the board. If they're talking too slowly, if it's boring, or if they're giving misinformation, you have to bring focus back quickly. You don't want students listening to a student drone on about something that isn't even accurate. If this happens, I say, "Well, actually, I disagree with you here. Let me explain why. But thank you so much for coming up and sharing your ideas."

We all clap for the student, and they return to their seat. If the student is doing a good job, however, then I let them stay up at the board as long as I can, because it's magical. Anytime you have students so pulled into the topic they come to the board to teach, you're winning.

SUPER-BOOST!
BECOME A BALLER

If you want to boost from one percent to five percent, teach your kids how to focus, no matter what. I created this game one day when kids were focused on talking but wouldn't listen to each other—they were just thinking about what they wanted to say. Finally, I got fed up. I said, "All right, everyone, put your hands down. No one can raise their hand. What I want you to do from now on is to track each other. Whenever someone is talking, I want you to *watch*." I started with a ball, and the person with the ball was allowed to speak. When they were done, they passed the ball to the next kid who had something to contribute. After about a week, they were able to track the lesson much better.

Now I make it into a game. "Kids, I have some friends coming into the class today, and they're going to try to distract you. If you lose focus—turn and look at them—they're going to tap you. That means you're out, and you go to the other side of the classroom. The game is to see who can keep following the lesson, even though it's going to be very distracting." I then have the staff come in wearing Halloween masks, and the kids try their best not to look at them. Sometimes they'll look, and then the teachers in the masks will tap them and say, "You're out." Finally, at the end, the custodian brings in the chainsaw and all hell breaks loose! I know it sounds a bit silly, but it's a fun way to hammer home the point of learning how to focus and track what everyone is saying.

19

WRITE A
HANDWRITTEN NOTE

Oh, the power of a handwritten note! Never underestimate its usefulness and versatility.

On the first Parent Night I did back in North Carolina, only four parents showed up. It broke my heart. So, before the next Parent Night, I sent each of the sixty-four parents cards saying, "I really hope you'll come next Tuesday to the Parent Night. It would mean so much." I handwrote those cards, and it meant a lot to people.

But the big difference was that they came to Parent Night, and we were able to open lines of communication that added to my understanding of their child and the parents' recognition of my hope to do the best for them. Nowadays, we're usually texting, copying, or emailing. But never forget how powerful a handwritten card can be.

Sometimes it can be hard to get parents involved. Once, Kim Bearden and I had an issue with a parent who wouldn't show up for meetings, wouldn't come to events, and wouldn't respond to anything that we sent. Finally, I said, "I'm going to just try a handwritten card. Maybe this will mean more to her."

"Good idea," Kim said. "I'll sign it. It'll come from both of us, letting her know that we appreciate her and that we'd love to hear from her."

So, we wrote the card. We let her know the parent meeting would be on Thursday at 3:00 p.m., and we'd love to see her there. It was important to talk about her child's progress. We were delighted when she showed up! She thanked us for the card and said, "I'm embarrassed to tell you we've had some issues and haven't had electricity at our home. So, I haven't been able to get on the internet, and I know I haven't been coming as much, but I really appreciated the card."

I felt terrible because I had been thinking this parent was ignoring us. Once I learned what was really going on, I recognized a new value in that handwritten card. It overcame a financial obstacle and helped me empathize with the parent and understand the child a little better.

Receiving a handwritten note is amazing, too. One year I asked our teachers to correspond with teachers from other schools who had been implementing our methods. I realized that one of our staff members, Korey Collins, had corresponded with not just some of the teachers at one of these schools but with *all* of the educators! I was so moved by this that I went online and bought him a *Star Wars* T-shirt with little Millennium Falcons on it. I wrapped it up and gave it to him with a card, noting that "The force is definitely with you!"

I didn't expect what happened next: Korey placed a handwritten card back in my mailbox, and it was incredible. He wrote about how grateful he was to be teaching at our school, how much it meant to him, and that he hadn't corresponded with the educators to get a shirt or a lovely card—he just did it because it was the right thing to do. That card meant so much to me.

If he had walked up to me and said, "Thanks for the shirt, I really appreciate it," it would've been nice, and I probably would have forgotten it by now. But there's something about that small effort of handwriting a card that goes a long way.

An educator visited RCA recently and later came up to me to say, "You won't remember this, but about eighteen years ago, I applied to work here."

"You did?"

"Yes, and you sent me a handwritten card that said, 'Thank you so much for applying. It's obvious you're a phenomenal teacher. I love the work that you do. Unfortunately, I don't feel like it's a fit right now for our school, but you are supremely talented, and I encourage you to keep up the amazing work—you're changing lives.'" Then I saw that she actually had that card in her hand! She added, "I just want to let you know I've kept it all these years because your note meant a lot to me."

You can never tell when you take a moment to share words on paper in your own handwriting how much it can mean to someone else.

TEACHER SHOUTOUT

BRANDIE MITCHELL
LIBERTY ELEMENTARY, SIOUX CITY, IA

After reconnecting with some former students during a walk-through-the-halls event with seniors, I decided a small but meaningful act I could do would be to send them all graduation cards with a quick note including some memories with them from first grade. It's a small way to keep the connection alive and let kids know I'm still rooting for them!

PERSONALIZE PARENT NIGHT

During Parent Nights, I love to use music from my own childhood to make connections. I once played an unexpected song when the parents came in—Pink Floyd's "Another Brick in the Wall." You know, the deep, dark, ominous song that goes, "We don't need no education."

As the parents sat down, I said, "You probably wonder why I was playing that song. Well, when I was a kid in the '70s, my dad was a DJ to raise extra money for our family at night. And every Saturday, he would go to the record store to buy the ten new records that had just been released. If you are old enough to remember, you know that when you bought ten, you got the eleventh one free. Well, my sister is five years older than me, and she always got the free record. But one week she had pneumonia, and it was the best week of my life. There I was, standing with my dad by ourselves in the record store, and I was thinking, 'Is he going to let me pick the free record?' Suddenly he looked down at me and said, 'Go on, pick it.' I didn't know what I was doing. I just reached for the one in the #1 spot, and my dad said, 'Good choice.' When I went home and played it, the scary, deep voice bellowed, 'WE DON'T NEED NO EDUCATION,' and I was like, 'Lord, the devil's in this record! What have I done?' But I learned every word, and now whenever it comes on the radio, I'm in that record store. I can still see my dad's sideburns. It means a lot to me."

Having parents see you as a human being with a history they can connect to means they're less likely to fuss at you or to send you a text message in all capital letters. You're a real person with feelings.

You're not just an anonymous teacher; you're an ex-kid, just like they are.

SUPER-BOOST!

TAKE-HOME TEST

Here's a real ten percent boost that supports parents helping their kids with a big upcoming test. Parents can be really daunted by their kids' schoolwork, so I put together a helpful practice test with support built in so parents don't feel lost.

Let's say a big math test is coming up. Make a practice test of around twenty pages. Cover all the content, and then give it to the parents. I usually say, "I want you to go home and give this test to your kid. Do one page a night, or two pages a night, or all of it in one night—whatever you want to do. Then you can grade it. That will let you know how your kid will do on the test next Friday."

The parents will ask, "Can we get an answer key?"

"Yes!" I say. "I've attached a twenty-page answer key. So, if your child misses a section, you can help them with that section." If parents ask, "What if I don't know how to help them with that section?" I show them I've written step-by-step content to demonstrate how to solve each problem.

I also add a section where I note common mistakes. So, a parent can see that if their child gets seventeen for the answer, it means she multiplied the exponent when she should have divided it. This helps the parents feel comfortable. They'll be able to say, "What were you thinking? You multiplied the exponent when you should have divided it." This at-home test also helps parents get a strong sense of their kid's strengths and weaknesses in various school subjects.

PULL THEM IN FROM THE FRINGES

At RCA, we have a regular activity in which we take pictures of each kid, enlarge the pictures, and put them on the floor in the gym. Teachers are given five red dots to place on the photos of the kids they're most connected to. You can then give five blue stickers for the next level of connection and then five yellow. I tell the staff that if they aren't really bonded or connected with any of the students, then they don't need to use all fifteen stickers. Afterward, the staff can look around the gym and see the relationships in the building in one big mosaic. As a group we then discuss which kids are not making teacher connections and think about ways to pull them into the fold.

Now, the dots exercise is useful (and if you have time to do it, I suggest you give it a try), but it's a lot of work. However, all it takes to pull shy or insecure kids into feeling that they are seen is to make a small effort every day.

Begin to call those kids' names more often in class or elsewhere in school. Maybe there's a kid on the basketball team who isn't great but gets in the game toward the end. You can go to the game and say to them later, "You know what? I think you were the key to why we won that game. You know when you ran to the right, and he got rattled? I think that's why he turned that ball over. I think that was a turning point in the game. You caused that. You won that game." It helps kids know I see them, that I'm cheering for them, and that I recognize they're part of the team as well.

There are loads of ways to make connections with sidelined students, to help them feel part of the larger group. Maybe three kids who are quiet and kind of isolated eat lunch together every day. I might think, "I'm going to buy them ice cream and tell them, 'I hope you all are having a good day.'"

If you see kids like these in the hall, smile at them more often, mention something they said in class, or ask them what their family did for a recent holiday. If you are looking for a bigger solution for seemingly lost kids, why not set up a luncheon with some of their teachers? It can be in a classroom away from the cafeteria, and you can have treats and games.

Once you start looking for these students, you will see them. And the satisfaction you'll get in pulling them in from the fringes will be matched by their appreciation. Just don't expect them to appreciate it out loud!

TEACHER SHOUTOUT

ERICA BLACK-VEAL
CHARLOTTE-MECKLENBURG SCHOOLS, CHARLOTTE, NC

Eat lunch with the kid that most students are not fond of and get to know them. Shine light on some of their accomplishments. True story—I did this with a student named Ryne. My class disliked him because of his sarcasm and personal hygiene, but I knew he had a wonderful relationship with his dad and uncle. I had the dad send me pictures of their fun-filled weekend. They went to a hockey game and had great seats. *None* of my students had ever been. I showed the class the pictures. They couldn't stop asking Ryne questions about the hockey game.

PERSUADE THEM WITH A PRESENT

The gift is on the table. It's in a big box, and it's wrapped beautifully. There's a large, red satin ribbon wrapped around the gift, just waiting to be untied. The gift has a big tag on it that reads, "For the amazing students in Mr. Clark's fifth-grade class." When kids walk into the class, they are shook!

And *they want that present.*

I've written about this before because this is one of my favorite lessons. I'm teaching about the art of persuasion. I'm telling students how politicians, salespersons, and commercials persuade the public with writing, speeches, and various tactics to make people think a certain way.

I'm tempting the students. That present is behind me, just sitting on my desk. Finally, the class wants to know what's in that present so desperately that they start to beg me. I let them know that I can't have them open the present, because they would be so excited that they would miss class time. I then add that I am sure they won't do double homework to make up for the missed class time. They then promise that they'll do double homework if I let them open it.

I let them open the present, and the present is . . . the double homework.

They'll say, "Mr. Clark, what is this?" They're always so shocked.

I point out, "I just persuaded you to make you think that you wanted whatever was in that box. I wrapped something you didn't want so prettily that you were desperate for it. How's that for persuasion?"

This is a very easy one percent lesson, because I already had the homework assignment ready. All I do is put it in a big box and wrap it beautifully. It only takes me five minutes, but the kids love it. "Oh, Mr. Clark tricked us. It was amazing."

I then encourage them to remember that moment for the rest of their lives so that they will learn to think for themselves and use better judgment.

HAVE THE MOST ABOVE-AVERAGE DAY EVER

Sometimes you should treat yourself by making life a little easier.

For example, every year at RCA we have this day called "The Best Day of School Ever." It's a lot of work, about a forty percent effort for everyone, but the kids absolutely love it. Normally, we pull all the kids into the auditorium, and I tell them we're going to have a full day of rigorous academic assessment to prepare for a state test. Then I add, "Or, we could just have the best day of school ever!" The kids go wild because they know what this is and that it happens once a year. It's a random day. They never know when it's going to happen, and students even want to come to school when they are sick so they won't miss it.

On this special day, buses pull up, and the kids, teachers, and staff all pile in. The buses then take them around the city to different spots where staff members are ready for them. For example, one year I was at State Farm Arena. When the bus pulled up with the seventh graders, they went into the arena, and I had the students use algebraic equations to figure out how many seats are in the entire arena. Then we shot at the basket, and they figured out the probability of making free throws. After thirty minutes, they got back on the bus and headed to the pool hall. Dr. Jones was waiting for them, and she had attached strings to corners on the pool table to teach them about how geometry can be found on a pool table and that if you understand geometry, you will be better at the game. It was really fun.

But, as you've probably guessed, setting up the day takes a lot of work. Well, that year during August preplanning, I asked the staff, "What day do you want to be the Best Day of School Ever?" We can do it whenever we want, because it's never placed on the calendar, and the students never know when it will be. The staff responded, "Let's do it in September so we can go ahead and get it over with." I didn't have a problem with that, but at the first staff meeting in September when I brought it up, someone said, "Can we please move it to October?" I said sure, but in October, they asked if we could move it to November. November is a short month because of Thanksgiving, so I suggested December. They all exclaimed, "Absolutely not!"

We kept putting it off until finally it was the end of the school year, and we still hadn't done it. I thought to myself, "Well, we can't do everything, and sometimes you have to let things go."

The next day I heard the eighth graders walking down the hall, and they were whispering, "We know it's tomorrow! It's got to be tomorrow."

Crap.

They hadn't forgotten. I told my staff that we had to dig deep and organize the Best Day of School Ever. They looked worn, but they accepted their fate as they said, "Okay. Let's do it."

Then I reconsidered. "Maybe we could aim to do an Above-Average Day of School."

I suggested, "Why don't we just make the announcement, get on the buses, and go to the park? Each of us can take a little container of whatever supplies we need. We'll teach underneath trees, and the kids can rotate between us. It's going to be seventy degrees next Thursday. We'll just sit under the trees, teach our lessons like we would in the classroom, but do it outdoors. We can email the parents as well and get a few of them to secretly show up and grill hot dogs and hamburgers."

The funny thing was, when we did it, it wasn't just an Above-Average Day of School. It was the Best Day of School EVER! Like seriously, in the history of the world, it may have been the best. We had an absolute blast.

First, the kids went wild. They loved it. We got to the park, and the weather was perfect. All the teachers positioned themselves around the park underneath trees, and as the students came to us for classes, they were attentive. We truly taught and got a lot accomplished. And the best part was the end of the day when the kids were saying it had been the best day of school ever. Even the teachers were saying it!

This made me realize that sometimes we feel we have to make a huge effort to make an impact. Instead of pulling out all the stops and asking everyone to give forty percent, sometimes it could be something much easier and much more manageable for the team. If you are thinking that you can't get buses to go to the park, or even take kids off campus, all you really need to do is just take your class outside for an hour at the end of the day and just teach there.

The kids will love it. I think they'd all get in the car afterward and say, "We had a great day. We had class outside."

Only you will know that really, you just made your life a little easier.

24

RECORD THAT REVIEW

This is a tip that will help you get a double benefit from work you're probably already doing.

We all want to provide our kids with the important information they'll need to review for tests. In order to help with this, during the last five minutes of a class, sometimes I'll take out my phone, plop it up on a desk right in front of me, and press record. As I am reviewing for the last five minutes of class, the phone is recording me while I'm saying something like, "All right, students, before you go, let's review one more time the five main reasons why the colonists won the Revolutionary War," or "Let's look at one more math problem so we can make sure that we understand what's going on." And then once the kids leave, I AirDrop that recording to my computer and put it on a learning management system the kids have access to, like Edpuzzle. When students go home, they can then watch the video if they need a review.

Sometimes I'll do a review by myself if the kids have already left, when I think they can use a little extra support. I'll pick the phone up and say, "Okay, let's review this Pythagorean theorem. I'm going to put an easy problem on the board. Press pause and try to solve it. Press play when you're ready. Let's now work it out together and see if you get it right."

I go through the lesson step by step, and the problems get progressively harder. I love these videos because students have access to reviews of important topics; and if the parents ask me later if I will tutor their child, I can say, "Well, they aren't even watching my videos." I'll know this because on Edpuzzle you can see who watched the video or not. You'll even be able to see how many times they watched it or if they watched only eighty percent of it.

If parents say, "My child says you talk too fast in class," I let them know about the videos and that they can rewatch videos and put me on slo-mo.

And for parents who want to help their children with their homework, they can watch the videos, too.

The most important part is that I have truly seen the videos help kids learn and master the content. The kids can understand your priorities and have a way to review content, at their own speed. Once you record some of these videos and post them, give each one a descriptive title, like "Area of a Triangle."

The beautiful part is in the double benefit: next year, all you have to do is go back to the platform and assign that video to your new class. Win-win!

25

SAY ONE NAME TO QUIET EVERYONE

I put down my fork and belted, "Hermione!"

The whole cafeteria went silent as students looked around for young Ms. Granger. I continued chatting with my colleagues.

This is a simple discipline trick I figured out early on. Sometimes I'll be in the cafeteria, and the kids are shouting and playing around—it's beginning to get chaotic. I just call out one name, loudly.

Obviously, teachers typically call out to the whole room, "Everyone, please be quiet!" And the room will get kind of quiet. They'll slowly, progressively get a little quieter; but they're still talking, and the noise level hasn't really gone down because they never entirely quieted down. However, if you want to make everyone be quiet instantly, just call *one* name—whether you're in your classroom or the cafeteria or the gym. If you call one name, everyone will instantly stop to find out what's up.

As I said before, you don't even have to call out the name of a kid in your school! If you're in the cafeteria, call out, "Samson, please! Samson!" Just call a name, any name. Everybody will quiet down, and then say, "Could you all please hold it down? Thank you." At that point the kids will be like, "Does a Samson even *go* here?" It's pretty funny, but more importantly, it works. And it might make them be quiet for longer, because they're trying to figure out who you were talking to.

However, in your actual classroom, you *have* to call a real name. I'll say, "Bernard, thank you. You're too loud." But by calling one name, you get everyone quiet; addressing "everyone" is never as successful.

26

TEACH THE IMPORTANCE OF HAVING AN AMAZING SHAKE

We need to take our students' lives outside of the classroom seriously. Years ago, I realized that academics are important, but if kids don't know how to go to an interview, shake someone's hand, fill out a job application, or use proper etiquette, they simply won't make it through the basic hurdles of life. Doors will shut in their faces, and they won't understand why. A lot of these kids think they're awesome, but falling at these first, basic hurdles can quickly drain their confidence.

I tell kids, "I want to prepare you for life. I want to let you know that there are some doors in your future that you're going to need to open, but you won't be able to open them because you don't have the keys. I want to give you the keys to these doors."

Kids should learn that the way you approach a person—whether you're going up to a bank teller or into a restaurant to ask for a table—will determine their reaction about fifty percent of the time. The other fifty percent, no matter what your approach is, you'll get the same response. But think about it! Fifty percent of the times you talk to someone, you can change the response you get. If you walk in there with a smile saying, "Hello, how are you doing? Good to see you. Hope you're having a great day," it opens a conversation and a connection.

Even if people look like they don't care about how you approach them, your effort goes a long way. I tell the kids, "Hold the door for someone. If you see trash on the floor, pick it up. If someone drops something, be the first one to rush to pick it up and hand it back to them." Common courtesies are important—pulling out a chair for someone, letting someone go ahead of you in line, little things like that.

It's important to teach kids these soft skills, these little one percent tips of life that open doors. I'm afraid there are kids who will apply for a promotion or a job, and they won't get it and won't understand why. A simple thing you can teach them is to dress well for an interview, to show that they care. People forgive inexperience, but indicating that you don't care (or don't understand how to show you care) is not forgivable.

Sometimes, adults aren't quite up to speed, either. I once had a candidate show up to an interview at RCA, and she was chewing gum. Instantly I thought, "I'm not hiring her. Why are you chewing gum? You can't come to an interview chewing bubblegum. Do you take this seriously?" Present yourself professionally. I honestly couldn't see past it, and she certainly didn't get the job.

On the flip side, our interview process was down to three candidates for a different position, and one of them sent the most lovely card and basket of dragon cookies as a thank-you for the interview. That sealed the deal for her; it was that little extra touch that won me over, and it was definitely the right choice. Dragon cookies don't lie.

If we don't teach our students these soft skills, like how to show appreciation and present themselves professionally or be courteous to the people around them, we are teaching them that it's okay not to take themselves seriously. That gives everyone they meet in the future permission not to take them seriously, either.

The Amazing Shake is a literal way of teaching your students to reach out in a courteous manner.

To help my students learn these soft skills, years ago I lined my whole staff up along the hallway and asked the students to go up to each staff member, give each of them a firm handshake, and introduce themselves. Beforehand, I showed the students how the squeeze should be firm, but not too firm—we practiced that firmness. I showed them how the thumb should press down when you're shaking someone's hand—a lot of people leave the thumb up.

I instruct students in a detailed manner because a good handshake can make or break an introduction. There should be an air pocket in the middle; the palms shouldn't be too flat. You've got to do a good, firm handshake, so we practice it. Then students go along the line and give every staff member a handshake, look them in the eyes, say their name, and say, "It's nice to meet you." The staff member takes the student's card and writes a score between one and ten on it. Then they turn it over, hand the card back to the kid, and the kid goes to the next person. When the student gets to the end of the line, they drop their card in a basket, not knowing what their scores were. After everyone has gone through the line, we calculate the scores and announce who had the best handshake in our school. We call it the Amazing Shake.

To make the lesson stick and ensure improvement among the low scorers, I say to the teachers, "Why don't we take the twenty lowest-scoring students and have lunch with them once a month? If they're not giving a firm handshake or making good eye contact, they need more social interaction." We set up lunch in a classroom, and once a month we eat with these students. We make eye contact. We help them with conversation. We teach them little things like putting a napkin in their lap that will help. Soon, we start to see a change in those students.

TEACHER SHOUTOUT

DR. ALEXIS MCKEEL
PS JONES MIDDLE SCHOOL, WASHINGTON, NC

My small improvement this year has been to teach students who drop into our office how to greet our amazing secretary if they haven't already. Most of our students have really caught on, and it's improved the atmosphere of our front office because they now greet our secretary every time they come to school. We were delighted this year when our rising fifth graders came over to make sure they knew our secretary's name and face so they could greet her in the future!

SUPER-BOOST!

HIGH-FLYING AMAZING SHAKE

This is a twenty percent boost that really has wings. After the first year we did the Amazing Shake at RCA, the students loved it and begged us to do it again the next year. I thought we should do it a little bigger, so I said, "Why don't we get business and community leaders from around Atlanta to come to RCA to serve as the judges?" So, we had twenty judges come. The kids got in a line not knowing these people at all, and these people didn't know the kids; the judging was objective. The students went down the line shaking the hand of each judge, and then they got their scores. This time it felt more like the real world because it wasn't their PE teacher's hand they were shaking. It was someone they didn't know.

The next year I expanded it further, figuring that we could help the students even more. We added a twist. Instead of just a handshake, we made sixty-second stations where the student would face a different challenge. At one station the student would interview with the vice president of Delta. He asked them, "So tell me why I should hire you to work here at Delta?" There was one challenge where students had to take a fork and a knife and cut a banana appropriately. In another, a student turned a corner to see a woman who had dropped a bunch of pencils. They had only sixty seconds to introduce themselves. Do they say, "Hello, my name is Ron?" Or do they say, "Oh, my goodness. Let me help you collect those pencils" and introduce themselves while they help? Do they have commonsense charisma? We reviewed best practices with the students beforehand.

The most beautiful part was that the judges gave real insight to the kids: "Here's what I was looking for. I liked how this student handled the situation." The students learned a lot and made real community connections.

But for those of you who are thinking this sounds like a lot of work, it starts as a one percent tip. Just start with your staff shaking their hands and discussing that basic skill. But it can grow, so this is going to be a boost if you want to do more.

If your school is interested in doing the Amazing Shake, we can give you everything you need. Just go to theamazingshake.com. You'll find videos to explain to you how to do it. All you have to do is reach out!

27

SHOW APPRECIATION, BUILD RELATIONSHIPS

Showing appreciation is an important life skill a lot of kids haven't been taught. They often receive something, and they don't write that handwritten note of gratitude. At RCA, students often ask us to write recommendation letters. And I've explained to the students, "I think you should handwrite the staff member you are requesting a recommendation from a card saying something like, 'Hey, Mr. Clark, would you be willing to write a recommendation letter? As a reminder, here's some great moments we've shared, or here's some of the activities that I participated in that you might want to include in the recommendation letter.'"

I don't ask students to do this because I am trying to make them jump through hoops or do extra work—I'm going to write the student the recommendation letter whether I receive that note or not. But it's a good habit for them to build because, when they go through life, showing appreciation for others' efforts is kind and actually increases the effort they put in.

Our staff member Korey Collins is fantastic at making people feel appreciated. Every time we do anything for the staff, he writes the most wonderful handwritten card and puts it on my computer. When I think of appreciation, I think of Korey Collins. And when I think of a staff member I want to do more for, I think of Korey because I know he's going to appreciate it because of that little card. If your boss does something for the team or takes you all out to lunch, if you're the one that writes the handwritten card, you're the one who has good social etiquette. You're the one who stands out. It's important.

I encourage my eighth graders as they leave my classroom to say, "Mr. Clark, thank you for the lesson. I really enjoyed it," or "Mr. Clark, I appreciate that I learned a lot today. Thank you." I tell them, "Some days my lesson isn't going to be that good, but you should still thank me because I'm trying to build something in you. When you go to high school or college and students walk out of those classes, I hope you will stay behind, walk up to the professor, and say, 'I really appreciated that lesson. Thank you.'" This goes a long way. Grading can be quite subjective when you're considering someone's writing, project, or effort. So, teach kids how to make the effort.

But always write the referral letters. Even if they don't present you with a card or formal request.

SUPER-BOOST!

BUILDING A SCHOOL, BUILDING THE GRATITUDE

Showing appreciation is important. It's how we built RCA. At the beginning of RCA, we couldn't get anyone to donate anything. All we had was this old, nasty factory, no money, and no students. Consequently, it was hard to explain the vision of what we were trying to build. I kept telling people that our school was going to be Scooby-Doo and magic and Harry Potter and flying dragons. People thought I was a lunatic. Maybe I was, but here's a Super-Boost tip on steps you can take to achieve a big goal and show gratitude for the support you received along the way.

First, I made a little booklet like a wedding registry with all the stuff donors, community members, and friends could buy for our school. The booklet contained hundreds of items like carpet for a math class, a toilet seat, or a kid's backpack. I had hundreds of items that supporters of the school could purchase, and I went to people, companies, and foundations all over Atlanta to ask, "Would you look through this little book and find something that you'd be willing to purchase?" Over a two-year period, more than three thousand people did. They purchased necessary school items, and that's how we built that school.

Afterward, my staff, our parents, our students, and I handwrote everybody thank-you letters. I couldn't write them all myself, so I had to get a big team. Every kind donor received a handwritten letter thanking them. And at Christmas I made sure those three thousand people all got a card. The postage cost a lot.

We made sure everyone got a card to let them know we were thinking about them. In the spring, I'd send them updates—funny little clips and things about the kids. Then for year two, we went back to those three thousand people and asked if they would be willing to support us again. Most said yes, and most of them contributed more than they did the year before. We built the school on relationships and letting people know that we appreciated them.

Someone once told me, "Teachers and schools are great at showing appreciation. They always send a lovely thank-you. But that's it. You don't hear from them again until they need something else. The reason why we give so much to your school is because you stay in contact, provide updates, and keep us connected." It goes a long way!

 **ERICA BLACK-VEAL**
CHARLOTTE-MECKLENBURG SCHOOLS, CHARLOTTE, NC

At the next school event, compliment a parent of a child not in your class for how supportive they are and how you like to see them in the school. Recognition and positive reinforcement build relationships!

28

BE POSITIVE ABOUT TEACHING AND LEARNING

At our school we have a lot of goals, but the main one is to make education dynamic and exciting and wonderful. Right now, our profession does not always feel that way. We have a shortage of three hundred thousand educators in America because many don't see our profession as enticing or joyful.

However, we want to attract the best people. And to do that, we don't have to make huge, time-consuming efforts. The first step to attracting great teachers is to be positive about teaching. Instead of saying anything bad about your school, only say good things. If you say ten good things about your school, they likely won't spread in the community. But if you say one bad thing, it will spread like wildfire. Maybe there is a great teacher considering joining your school, and she says to a friend, "I'm thinking of applying there." The friend may say, "I've heard bad things about them." Then, the great teacher doesn't even apply to your school. You've caused that.

I tell my staff that we should never put critical things on Facebook. Have you ever seen the meme about a rat that's drowning? Some teachers post it and write, "This is me as a teacher on Fridays." And people laugh at it and share it. But I think about how I want to delete the post because it's bad publicity. If we want our profession to be seen as young, fun, and dynamic, we have to publicize our profession better. Don't post those "funny" memes. Don't count down how many days there are left to the break. People see it. It's a simple one percent way to contribute to something greater than yourself.

When we spend time on university campuses and we try to encourage college students to become teachers, they say, "I've heard horror stories."

There are so many small, meaningful things you can do to shed a bright light on the educational profession. First, instead of posting something cool that you're doing in your classroom on social media, post about another teacher's activities. It's an awesome, huge boost if you can highlight something a colleague is doing by giving them a shout-out and letting the world see the great work they do. (First ask your colleague if it's okay; some people might not want to be highlighted on social media.) Putting a spotlight on our colleagues' strengths is a wonderful way to spread good news about our profession.

Second, if any of your students say they want to be a teacher, respond with encouragement! Tell them they're going to be a wonderful educator, and tell them all the satisfying things about teaching. Why spread negative energy about the work that we do? All it does is make the work harder and perpetuate our culture's deprioritization of education.

It breaks my heart when we go to college campuses to encourage students to become teachers, and the best response we get is, "Oh, I'm going to consider it. If nothing else works out, then I'll definitely consider teaching."

That's who we are attracting in our profession. People who see it as a last resort if nothing else works out. We've got to do a better job of highlighting how our profession is a fun and profoundly meaningful way to spend your professional life.

Another thing you can do in your school to promote positivity is cheer for a colleague if they win an award! Celebrate your colleagues and their successes. Be genuinely happy for them. I know you may have wanted that award, but it wasn't for you this time. Or maybe you thought someone else deserved it, but it didn't work out for them, either.

So, you have two options. You can pout and be negative about someone's success, or you can cheer for them, celebrate them, and uplift them. You may not even like them or their teaching style very much. They use too much glitter, or they're too perky for you; but this is bigger than you, and it's bigger than your issues with perkiness. It's about celebrating the profession and doing all we can to shine a bright light on its importance and its successes.

Another one percent thing you can do is defend a colleague if you hear a student say something negative about them. For example, if a kid says, "I don't like Ms. Williams. She's boring," you may quite honestly think that Ms. Williams is boring. You may think she's a bad teacher. You may not like Ms. Williams. But when that child says, "Ms. Williams is boring," don't say, "I know, just do the best you can. Not all teachers have the same philosophy of teaching." Instead, say to the student, "I don't think you understand how hard Ms. Williams works for you, and you're going to pay attention for her. You're not going to talk badly about anyone in this building in front of me. Am I clear?"

Let those students know that you are not the one to talk to when it comes to negativity about other teachers. You want to spread positive energy. In our school, I tell my staff to say nothing but good things about their colleagues. Cut the gossip and the pointing fingers because all it does is spread a culture of dissatisfaction. And you never know what's going on behind closed doors.

For example, say there's a teacher at your school who has started leaving at two o'clock every day. Where is she going? Why does *she* get to leave early while you labor on? It bothers you. Well, that's not your responsibility. Maybe that teacher is lazy—in which case she'll eventually be held responsible. Or maybe that teacher has a spouse who is undergoing chemotherapy, and they need to drive them there.

Or maybe their parent has an ongoing medical issue. You simply never know about others' lives, and spreading negative assumptions just wastes everybody's time. Keep your side of the street clean and shine a light on colleagues who are excelling.

We are all too busy for the negativity. We have to teach all day. We have families at home. There's a lot to deal with in all our lives. So, don't add other people's mistakes to the list. The errors of others are not something else that you need to add to your shoulders. You're *choosing* to add that to your shoulders. It's my job as an administrator to worry about others' faults. You don't have to write that teacher up; you don't have to do her observation—I do that. You just need to be kind to her, and that's all I'm expecting of you. Be kind and don't gossip. You don't need to know what's going on with her. It's not your business.

We must do a better job of showing the good things in education because there are great things about our profession. On your website, if I go to apply to work at your school, just listing the names of your staff and their emails seems cold to me. But if someone on your team goes around and takes a photo of every staff member and puts the picture by their name and email address, along with their favorite movie, that school cares about people. That feels like a warm, inviting place.

Your school needs to be a positive, fun place—and people need to know it!

HALF PERCENT BOOST
DON'T BRING NEGATIVITY HOME WITH YOU

When you go home at the end of the day, remember that we want our spouses to look forward to us returning home! If we walk in and immediately start complaining about what happened at school, our spouses will begin to dread our return each day.

Instead of complaining, come in and give your spouse a kiss on the lips. Now, you don't have to tongue kiss, but at least give them a peck. Tell them something good about your day, because every day has something good. Maybe a little later, if you want to share a few negative things and get some advice, that's fine. But try not to start unloading the moment you walk in the door because your spouse will start to resent your job.

If you come home and talk about how much you can't stand the principal, then a few days later say you volunteered to help that principal at a bake-a-thon, your spouse will say, "Why would you go help her after what she did to you this week?" They will start to resent the job. If you've complained about the students, your spouse might wonder, "Why are you baking cookies for those kids if they were so rude to you? They don't deserve those cookies."

So, remember that when you're sharing negativity, it can cause people who love you to dislike your job or resent the people you work with. This is just creating trouble in the future. We need to be truthful with our spouses, and Lord knows sometimes we need support. But be mindful of not painting your job as a horrible place if actually most of the time it's wonderful.

INVITE A REALTOR TO YOUR SCHOOL

Who (apart from teachers) gets to meet the most people in your community?

Maybe the chapter title gave it away. But yes, it's real estate agents!

So, invite them to visit your school. When people want to move to your town, they'll ask real estate agents, "What's the school like?" If the agent's never been to your school, they might not have great things to say, or maybe they'll have nothing to say. But what if you invite real estate agents to come, have four or five students greet them in the lobby, give them firm handshakes, and offer them a little tour of the school? Ask the students to take the real estate agents to watch your best teacher teach. (Just the best one.) Then invite the real estate agents to sit down and have a snack or lunch with the students.

What you want is to be sure that later, when someone asks, "What's the school like in this neighborhood," the real estate agent will say, "Oh, well, I was just there last week, and it blew me away. What wonderful kids and teachers."

Real estate agents meet such a large percentage of your community that they can boost or sink your school's reputation. So, take a little time to make them your community-wide boosters!

SUPPORT YOUR COLLEAGUES' EXCELLENCE

When someone on your staff does something awesome or one of your colleagues goes above and beyond, let them know it. Go over to them and say, "That lesson looked amazing. You are a fantastic teacher. I'm honored to work with you."

Or maybe you can say, "I saw you tutoring that child yesterday. That child is not easy to like. Thank you so much for the time you spent with her." When you give colleagues kudos, you are not only giving them the freedom to do more things like that but you're also counteracting the negativity. Because I can almost assure you that someone in that building has said something like, "Oh, here you go again. Lord, have mercy. You're doing too much." You are counteracting that negativity by letting them know they should do more.

You could even do it right now, as you're reading this book. Put the book down (and I hope you do), pick up your phone, and text someone you work with who is not your best buddy—they already know you admire them. Text another colleague and say, "I just want to let you know, I think you're a great teacher, and I appreciate the effort that you put into your lessons." Or maybe they're not really that great, but they *do* something great. Maybe they teach the volcano lesson brilliantly. Just text them and say, "I was just thinking about that volcano lesson you do with your students. That's so cool how you do that. They'll never forget that for the rest of their lives. You're awesome!"

And who knows? They might think, "Oh, people are actually noticing my volcano lesson!" So maybe next time they'll make volcanoes and clouds, and the clouds will produce rain, and the volcano explodes all over the classroom. I bet if you sent them that text, the next time they teach that lesson, it will be even bigger and better. And once they know their efforts are being recognized, it might encourage them to improve the other facets of their job as well.

This is how we need to uplift each other. This is how we can make our profession feel more young, fun, and dynamic—and how we can attract more people to our profession. Another one percent tip you can do is high-five your colleagues. If you feel comfortable, hug them. Laugh with them in the hallway. A lot of the students we teach come from really challenging backgrounds. Students deal with a lot of issues that we don't know about. So, when you laugh with colleagues and that laughter fills the hallway, that sense of joy can change the entire climate and culture of your school and make it a place where students look forward to spending their time.

We need to make the profession of teaching fun again; we need to make it something that makes us feel happy and as if our work has great meaning. Because it truly does—but we need to remind each other of just how fantastic we are.

So, get out there and give someone a well-deserved boost!

HALF PERCENT BOOST
SCRATCH ON, SCRATCH OFF

A little thing I like to do for my staff to have some fun and show appreciation is buy them all two-dollar lottery scratch-offs. When they come to a faculty meeting, I have "Eye of the Tiger" playing. Everyone comes in, and there are scratch-offs and coins waiting for them. They all scratch off their tickets. It's just a fun way to start the meeting, and they love it. I don't do it too often, just when I feel my staff can use a little pick-me-up.

GIVE KIDS
A CHOICE

Here's a way to inject energy into your class: give kids a choice in how they learn. Or what they learn. Or *where* they learn. What matters is that the students make decisions in your classroom.

For example, I might say, "All right, we have ten minutes left in class. Let's take a vote. Who wants to review the math problems? Who wants to do the quizzes game? Or who wants to have a multiplication fact game-off?" Then I let them choose. Kids love when they get a vote, and they all tend to really get into that last ten-minute thing.

Because let's face it, if I just said, "We're doing quizzes in the last ten minutes," there'd be zero enthusiasm. But when I let them vote, they get to choose. It gives them some autonomy. In your class, occasionally give them that autonomy. For example, it could be something simple. Maybe you say, "Hey, tonight for homework, you can do this assignment or this one. What do y'all think? Let's take a vote." And then you all decide on what the assignment is. Giving them that voice in the classroom goes a long way. Kids like it because they feel respected. They feel seen; they feel heard. It's important.

We have a wheel in our school that we spin to make some decisions for us. For example, one time we had a donor who offered to send our honor roll students—there were twenty-three of them—on an all-expenses-paid trip with staff members to *anywhere* in the Western Hemisphere they wanted to go. I was so excited.

I kept saying, "Kids, we're going to Brazil. We're going to Costa Rica. Where are we going?" But I also told the kids they could choose, even though I personally had a million dream destinations, especially locations in South America.

It's important to let the students have autonomy. They met to discuss their options, and I asked for their decision.

"We decided, Mr. Clark, that we want to go to the Grand Canyon."

"Huh?" I said. "The Grand Canyon? We can do that some other time. Let's go to Brazil." I never said it was easy giving kids a choice. Or that it came naturally to me.

"No, Mr. Clark," they responded, "Grand Canyon! Grand Canyon!"

"No, seriously, everyone. We can go to the Bahamas. We can go snorkeling. Why would we go to the Grand Canyon?"

"We saw a book on the Grand Canyon in the library, and we really liked it. It looks beautiful."

"Oh, yes," I said, "it's beautiful. It's a natural wonder. But Brazil. We could get to go to Brazil. Do you understand? We can go to the Grand Canyon whenever we want."

But they were determined on the Grand Canyon.

Finally, I said, "You know what? Why don't we let the wheel decide?" We headed to the wheel and decided to make our options— the Grand Canyon, the Bahamas, Costa Rica, and Brazil—correspond to the four sections on the wheel. We spun the wheel, and I couldn't help but notice that, as the wheel was spinning, the kids were chanting, "Grand Canyon, Grand Canyon, Grand Canyon!"

Before the wheel even stopped, I said, "Okay, everyone. You know what? Forget it. No matter where it stops, we're going to the Grand Canyon." The kids cheered—and guess where that wheel landed? Of course, on the Grand Canyon. Those kids were so elated.

Thanks to support from our donors, students from our school travel every year. We've gone to Japan, to England, and all over the world: Kenya, South Africa, Egypt, China, Greece, Spain.

Of all the places we've been, my absolute favorite trip was that one I didn't want to take.

That's right, the Grand Canyon. Have you been? It's *fascinating*. All I could think was, "How does everyone in the world not go here?" We went whitewater rafting and camped out under the stars. It's just gorgeous and peaceful and beautiful. And the stars at night—you see the whole Milky Way. Plus, we told ghost stories. We had a blast.

The kids were right. Sometimes letting the kids have autonomy, letting them have a choice, allows us to learn. Adults don't always know best, even if it means we miss out on going to Brazil.

32

GET DRESSED UP

My mom told me, "We don't have money for a costume."

But I *had* to find a costume. My fifth-grade teacher, Ms. Edwards, was letting us dress up for Halloween! So, my mom and I figured something out. My mom took a sheet, cut a hole in it, and put it over my head. Then she put some gel in my hair and took her mascara and drew some scars on my face and put some glasses on me. I was a mad scientist! I will always vividly remember that day. I remember when we

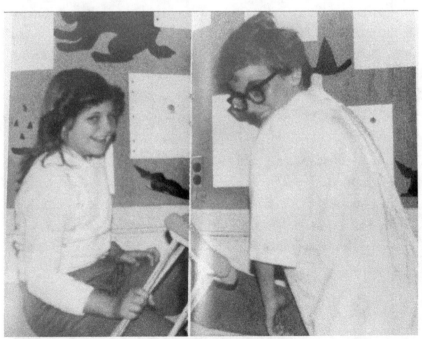

Here I am in the fifth grade in my homemade "mad doctor" costume. I was pretending to take care of Julie Beavers's leg. It was simple, and my mom just threw it together, but somehow, I won the costume contest award.

got to school; I remember how the math lesson started. I was sitting there, feeling proud. I was in a costume. I felt different, unique.

Why not let your kids dress up sometimes? Little things like that let kids express something and feel excited about the upcoming day.

Kids absolutely love to dress up. I'll never forget the first thing I ever heard about the cofounder of RCA, Kim Bearden. I read an article that said that when she was teaching descriptive writing, she set up a runway in the middle of her classroom and had her students bring all types of gaudy clothes from home. They put on these mismatched clothes and held a fashion show. The students had to write an article describing their outfit, and they had to be as descriptive as possible in detailing the ridiculousness of the clothing that they were wearing. It was just so clever! The students brought old coats and gloves and socks and dresses and scarves from home, and they put all of it on to walk the runway. I bet those students will never forget that activity. It's just fun to dress up, whatever your age—but kids particularly love it.

We have different houses in our school, and one of them is Rêveur; their color is blue, and their mascot is a wolf. I'm in that house, and I bleed blue! We're the dreamers, and we howl at the moon just like our mascot. So, one year I ordered every kid in Rêveur a wolf costume—I even ordered their parents wolf costumes as well!

Now, whenever we have an opportunity at an event, everyone comes in wolf onesies; it's hilarious. This exercise had an interesting extension. A few students said, "Mr. Clark, we're the wolves. We howl at the moon. But we've never seen the moon before." That struck me as a thing we could fix, so we took those kids camping deep in the woods to howl at the moon. When we were standing there looking up at the moon and howling, one of the kids said, "Mr. Clark, I haven't ever seen stars before."

We all live in Atlanta, so you can see stars occasionally, but they're only poking through the city's light pollution. You barely see them. But when we were standing there in the middle of the woods, you could see the entire Milky Way, and the kids' eyes were open wide. It was a powerful moment. And there we were standing in our wolf costumes, even the parents.

But some wolves are built different.

Another easy thing you can do to highlight your house system is sew house patches on your pants, your coats, or your jacket. Every town has a tailor (or a parent could do it), and adding patches for seven or eight dollars goes a long way to spice up your attire and personalize it for your house or school.

In addition, we have a holiday feast every year at Christmas, and it's a tradition that I will dress up for the meal as a different character. I have dressed up as all sorts of mean characters; the students absolutely love it. I walk around wreaking havoc at the lunch, throwing people's food away, flirting with grandmas, and bringing hilarity to the event. It's a wonderful way to add a spark of magic to the event!

33

SPEND A LITTLE TO GET A LOT

Sometimes, a person's one percent extra can translate into something big.

In our gym at RCA, we have a huge, beautiful tapestry of our students. Every four years, we make a new tapestry after all of the students in the tapestry have graduated. This year, we were due to make a new tapestry, so I called a local company, Cady Studios, to schedule a photographer.

When I called, they said, "Oh, Ron, just to let you know, I know we've charged you and your sponsor $8,000 in the past, but supply chain issues have increased costs. So, the tapestry is now $16,000."

"Sixteen thousand dollars?" I said. "I don't have $16,000."

"Well, I'm sure you'll be able to find a way and raise the funds."

I'm good with people, so I tried to appeal to their emotions. "Think of the children," I said. "These kids are going to be devastated if they don't see their faces on this wall."

"We're so sorry," they replied, "but we can't change the price." I had to accept it.

After I heard the new price, I told the staff we weren't going to make a new tapestry. But they disagreed: "We *have* to do it. All those kids have graduated."

"Well, we just don't have the $16,000," I said.

"We have to find it."

"Well, I don't have time to find another $8,000. We have so much to do. We'll just change it next year. I'll work next year to get another donation."

Well, Cady Studios would not leave me alone. They kept emailing, calling, and texting me: "Hey Ron, we'd love to come do this wall. It's just $16,000 to change the climate and culture of your school."

I kept writing back, "We'd be happy to pay you $8,000, but that's all we have."

But then on a Friday, Stephanie from Cady Studios emailed me and said, "Hey Ron, we'd love to come and do your tapestry for you. If you could meet with me on Monday to sign the contract, I could be there at 9:00 a.m., and I'd be happy to bring you your favorite morning beverage."

Morning beverage?

I was shook by that.

Morning beverage.

I don't even drink coffee.

I sat there for a moment, and then I wrote back, "Okay."

Everybody else was telling me, "We need to do the wall. Do the wall. Do the wall." But Stephanie said, "I'd love to come meet with you and bring you your favorite morning beverage." I guess I just respected the little extra she was giving me. It was her one percent, and it spoke to me.

When she came on Monday, I signed that contract. I didn't push back. I signed the contract for $16,000. I had to go to a board meeting afterward, and after I explained the story, my board president said, "Ron, that was a very expensive cup of coffee." I replied, "I know, but I couldn't help myself."

Kind gestures go far in life for a teacher, or for anyone.

We had a family we wanted to come visit RCA, and we hoped they'd become donors. As we were trying to get them to come visit the academy, they let us know that they had other nonprofits they support, and they really weren't open to adding another school to their list. But they applauded our work from afar.

"Well, we understand that you won't be donors," I told them, "but would you consider visiting anyway?"

"Sure," they said, "we'd love to visit and see what you do. We won't be able to add you to our donor list, but we'd love to visit."

They were in New York City at the time, planning to see the Broadway show *Wicked*. I told my staff, "They're in New York City now, and they're coming through Atlanta on Friday. They'll be in town for one night. Here's what I want you to do. Call every hotel in Atlanta and find out where they're staying. Start with the ritzy places because they have money."

One of my staff, Kirk Brown, suggested, "I can just call them back and ask where they're staying."

"We can't do that," I said. "We *have* to find out on our own. I want a *Wicked* basket with green cellophane inside their room waiting for them when they arrive. I want *Wicked* cookies, *Wicked* T-shirts. I want all kinds of *Wicked* stuff in there. And let's have a card saying, 'We hope you had a wickedly good time in New York City and that you will have an equally great time when you visit RCA.'"

Kirk said, "Where do we even get *Wicked* cookies?"

I replied, "I have no idea. Ask the parents to bake them."

This basket ended up costing us $300, but it was waiting for them in their hotel room. When the family walked into our school the next day, all they could talk about was the *Wicked* basket. "That *Wicked* basket that was so thoughtful. How'd you find our hotel? And that card, that was so . . ." They just kept going on and on. At the end of the tour, they let us know that they would become one of our donors.

They wanted to support us, and they've grown to be one of the biggest supporters of the school, and it all started with that *Wicked* basket.

See, I made up for the expensive cup of coffee fifty times over with a one percent *Wicked* basket.

Common courtesies, the extra mile, just doing something unexpected that you don't have to do but you want to—these little things can make a world of difference.

SET STANDARDS
(AND STICK TO THEM)

How would you respond to this scenario?

You're teaching a kid who gets mad, pulls a pencil out, and stabs another kid in the arm with it, leaving a mark on the kid's arm. A little piece of the lead went into the second kid's arm. What do you think the consequence should be for the kid with the pencil?

I've asked this question of countless educators, and I get a variety of answers. Using restorative practices, you would find out the root cause of the problem. These teachers ask the kid why they stabbed his classmate and what brought it on. And then some teachers say, "I don't care why they did it. That kid needs to be suspended. That kid could be expelled. That kid needs to be sent home immediately for ten days." Others say, "Just make the kid apologize." And some will say, "Call the kid's mother."

The point I'm making is that all over the country and the world, punishment for the same infraction could be handled a million different ways. But what ends up happening in your school when you have inconsistency with discipline—i.e., one teacher handles something one way, and the teacher across the hall handles it another way—is that kids begin to feel that things aren't fair. If you have multiple teachers who are strict and abide by the rules, and one teacher is loosey-goosey, the kids start to think that the strict teachers are mean and the loosey-goosey teacher is nice. So, if you're the loosey-goosey teacher, you're causing problems. But if *everyone* is strict and they follow set expectations, no one is mean.

It's all about the expectations you set up and how closely you adhere to them.

When I came up with the Essential 55 Rules I taught my students in New York City, I covered everything from how to turn in your homework and how to treat each other to how to respect me as a teacher. Once I'd taught the rules and role-played them, one of the kids said, "Mr. Clark, I like this class now. Nobody's bothering me. I can focus and get my learning on."

I thought, "Buddy, you were the worst one. What are you talking about?" But I realized in that moment that every kid wants discipline. Every kid wants structure. Every kid wants to know that you're in charge. They want to know that you have the class under control. And if they realize that you don't have the class under control, they're going to get anxious and take control themselves.

They'll get loud. They'll start to pick on other kids because, when you don't have control, they feel uneasy. They feel out of control. They don't feel safe in the environment. They will become the aggressors; they'll become the alphas. And when several of them do that, that's when you've lost complete control of your classroom. Really, it starts when you don't have control of (or confidence in) yourself.

At RCA, I felt that we needed to start by having complete control. The administration and staff had to make sure that we were consistent. As a staff, we sat down and went through scenarios like this one. What should we do if a kid doesn't have a pencil? Some staff members will say, "Give them one."

"How much money are you spending on pencils a year?" I ask.

Every time I go into a classroom where the teacher gives pencils away, there are pencils all over the floor. At the end of the day, they just get a free pencil every time they want one, so kids don't respect the pencil. You're not teaching them a life lesson.

Here's what I do. I tell the kids, "If you don't have a pencil and no one in the class will give you one, you get detention." In thirty years, I've never had a kid actually get the detention; someone will always hand them a pencil.

But what if I'm handling it that way, and there's a teacher down the hall who does it a little differently?

"Oh, I'll give them a pencil, but they have to give me a shoe," one teacher told me.

"What?"

The teacher nodded. "Yeah, they have to give me their shoe. Then they get the shoe back after they give me the pencil back."

"I don't think kids would like that very much," I said. "Some kids are funny about their shoes. They would probably find you mean, especially when the teacher across the hall is giving away pencils for free." This made me realize that we had to come up with a consistent school-wide plan.

Bullying is a big issue in kids' lives now. So, what do you do in your class if a kid calls another kid stupid? What should you say? Is there a set discipline? A silent lunch? A detention? A call to Mom? An apology? How severe is that? What should we do?

This usually happens in the first week of school with the fourth graders, who are new to the school. If a kid calls another kid stupid, I'll stop the class and say, "All right everybody, he just called her stupid. What should you all have done about it?"

The kids say, "Mind our business."

"No."

Then they'll suggest, "We should do nothing."

I shake my head. "No, no, no. If he calls her stupid . . ."

"Should we look away?"

"No. If he calls her stupid, you all need to take up for her and say, 'Hey, hey, no.' You all have to say that to him at the same time. That it isn't cool. We don't do that here. He'll back down, because if you let him call her stupid today, tomorrow *you're* going to be stupid. And then the next week he's going to have some other names for you. And then you have a full-on bully in the class. If you stand up to him now, you will be able to focus on your learning. So don't let bullying happen. Because they'll stop when all of you say, 'That's not cool. We don't do that here.' And if you giggle when the bully calls someone a name, you're feeding the dragon. Odds are you're going to be the one that gets the fire later."

You need to have these conversations with your staff so you have continuity throughout your building. What do you do if a kid in your school breaks line? Is there an offense for that? What if a kid cheats on a test? What if a kid uses a curse word? What if a kid steals something from another kid? What if a kid uses their cell phone in class? What if a kid comments on another kid's appearance, saying they're fat or their nose is too big? What are the consequences? What if you see a boy chasing another boy around the bathroom; they're both laughing, but the one who's chasing the other has his fist clenched. What are the consequences? Do you just tell everyone to get to class, or do you refer them to the office? Or do you call their moms? Ask your staff what they think and have them write down what they think the consequence should be. Then have them share.

You will learn that everyone in your building would do something different. That's why these conversations and planned consistency are important. You all must get on the same page.

This means having a conversation with your staff where you go through typical scenarios and come to a consensus on how those situations should be handled. I'm calling it a one percent effort here because it only takes about thirty minutes. You're trying to gain some consensus and get an idea of the thought process of your team. As an administrator, you're guiding the thought process by saying, "After hearing everyone, this is how I recommend we handle the situation moving forward." It goes a long way to provide clarity and get everyone on the same page.

And hopefully it will go a long way to making sure students' pencils are used only for writing.

DO A TEN-MINUTE JOURNAL

Every day, my sixth-grade teacher, Mrs. Walker, had us write in our journals for ten minutes. We would sit at our desks and scribble on about our weekends or upcoming plans. And every Tuesday after school, she would stay and read every journal and write comments. She would write something like, "Oh, I enjoyed your story. Good luck at the party this weekend!"

I'll never forget how I couldn't wait to get to school every morning on Wednesday. I'd be so excited to get to school on those days because I wanted to see what she wrote my journal. Did she read it? What did she say?

One time I wrote about how I was going to someone's wedding, and my family didn't have money like the people who were having the reception. It was a fancy wedding, and I was really looking forward to it. Mrs. Walker wrote a comment referencing something about the fiancé. And I wrote back, saying, "Oh, Mrs. Walker, don't worry about it. They're very rich. Their fiancé's fine." I thought she meant finances. She just wrote back, "Ha, ha, ha." It's still so funny to me that I thought she meant finances.

That was almost forty years ago, and I still remember that exchange. It was her way of taking a moment to let me know that she saw me.

Sometimes it's hard to show each child attention because there are so many kids, but it's meaningful to create that small interaction with each of them. Little things like that go a long way. The connection she built through those journals built a lasting memory for me—I bet it did for many more of her students.

LEARN TO FORGIVE

If you want to be a great eighth-grade teacher, you have to learn forgiveness.

You have to learn to forgive the kids, because eighth graders are a real mess. They don't know what they're doing. You must learn to forgive them because they will hurt your feelings.

Of course, kids in other grades will hurt your feelings, too, but those eighth graders can be something. Regardless of the grade level, however, learn how to handle it, because there might—just *might*—be payoff later.

I had this student named Wade Medford. He was a great kid and the star of our school musical. One time we took a trip to Nevada with some students to go to a ranch. We had to drive five hours to get to this ranch. Our plane landed late at night, and I had to drive a car there, even though I was dead tired. So, myself and three kids got in a car to follow a bus with the rest of the students. Wade was sitting beside me in the passenger seat, and the two other kids were in the back asleep.

For five hours, Wade talked to me the whole time. I thought, "Thank goodness for him." I would've fallen asleep. We just talked and talked and talked and talked and laughed. Somewhere along the journey, one of the kids in the back, Malachi, woke up and said, "Mr. Clark, I have to go to the bathroom."

"Buddy, we're in the middle of nowhere. You're going to have to go to a tree or something. I'll pull over. You can find somewhere to go." Then I saw a porta potty on the side of the road. I pulled over, and on the side of the porta potty, it said Honey Bucket. That cracked us up—a porta potty called Honey Bucket. So, Malachi went to use the bathroom, and Wade said, "Mr. Clark, we should go scare him and shake the Honey Bucket." I agreed. We took off running, and we shook the Honey Bucket and made bear noises. Malachi screamed on the inside, and we laughed.

For years afterward, we kept making Honey Bucket jokes. We thought it was hilarious.

Years later, after Wade had graduated and gone on to high school, I went into a Kilwins store at Atlantic Station and saw him there with a friend of his. I hadn't seen Wade in over a year. So, I called over to him, "Wade." Wade looked over, then he looked away like he didn't see me. High school kids can be too cool for anything, but I said, "Wade, it's Mr. Clark."

Wade said, "Oh. Oh. Okay, hey." Then he turned away back to his friend and started trying to walk away, like he was embarrassed with this old teacher saying hello.

It broke my heart. I had a rough time that day. It can be rough to forgive kids because sometimes we feel we've bonded with them, but they may not feel the same way. He was a great kid, one of my favorite students. And he was embarrassed to say hello to me.

Years later, I got a phone call. It was Wade. "Hey, Mr. Clark, I'm graduating from Georgia Tech."

"I know, Wade. I'm so proud of you."

"They only give three tickets to the graduation," Wade said. "I have a big family, but I'm asking my mom, my dad, and I was wondering if you would come and take that third ticket."

Immediately I said, "I'd love to, Wade. Of course I'll be there."

Perhaps he felt guilty because of what happened in the Kilwins. Maybe he had been thinking about it all those years. I think he felt he had to make it up to me. And that's how he did it. I believe it's important to forgive kids because they don't know what they do. And the beautiful part is when they do realize, they come around in the end. And you better believe, I was the loudest one cheering at his graduation!

37

USE COMMONSENSE CHARISMA

It's so easy to half-listen to people or half-see them, particularly when we're stressed, busy, or tired. But it means we miss big opportunities to make connections and have fun.

I've come up with a phrase to remind people to bring their whole person to each interaction: commonsense charisma.

I tell students that if you want to have this commonsense charisma, lock eyes with a person when you're talking to them. Never look around the room or down at your shoes. Everyone will think you're trying to get away from the conversation and you're not truly paying attention to them.

Part of this charisma is also knowing when to let people go. If you're talking to someone and you've locked eyes with them, and you notice their eyes darting around the room, that's a commonsense clue to let you know they want the conversation to end or there's someone else they need to go speak with. You don't want to prolong the conversation because that will just annoy the person. So go ahead and let them know it was nice talking with them and let them go.

Another commonsense tip: many people don't understand that when you're having a conversation, other folks don't really want to hear about your problems or how tired you are. They want to tell you *their* problems and how tired *they* are.

So, if you *have* to share a problem or tell someone how tired you are, keep it brief and to the point. How is this charismatic? Well, people love stopping to chat with someone they know won't trap them for an involved complaining session.

It's also common sense to realize you've found a seriously good friend when that person will happily listen to your problems and issues for as long as you want. It's common sense to make sure you give them time to vent, too.

Commonsense charisma in a sense is just a natural ability to connect with others in an intuitive and empathetic way. It deals with having a grounded, relatable demeanor that makes individuals feel that you are approachable and trustworthy.

Here's an example. We recently had a major foundation come to RCA, and we were stressed out about it. So right before they came, I began playing around a little bit. All the middle school kids at our school try to jump and hit a high bar when they head into the hallway. I said to my staff members who were about to greet the foundation, "I wonder if I could hit that bar." So, I jumped and hit the bar. Then my colleague Troy Kemp jumped and hit the bar. Kirk Brown jumped and hit the bar. Kim Bearden jumped and hit the bar.

Then I said, "I wonder if we could hit the brick above the bar." So, we all started backing up and trying to see if we could jump and touch that brick. We were having a blast. Then the students came out. I don't know if any of you teach eighth-grade boys, but the pinnacle of their existence is to jump and hit something. They thought it was hilarious. It was silly. It was fun. We were laughing, jumping, and hitting that thing. And it wasn't orchestrated. It just happened because we made room for it by prioritizing laughter. Bring the joy. Your students want to see you enjoying yourselves. It brings a lightness to their day just to see you enjoying, laughing, and joking with each other. It doesn't take much effort, and the returns lighten the day for everyone.

I turned and saw that the leaders of the foundation were walking in the front door. (Not to name-drop, but it was the leaders of the Oprah Winfrey Foundation, and it was their first visit to RCA.) They'd seen us playing this silly game, running and jumping and trying to hit the brick. We went over to them laughing and said, "We don't know if you know much about middle school kids, but they have this thing about jumping and seeing what they can touch. We were all trying. Would y'all like to try?"

Pretty soon, they were trying to jump and hit the bar and then the brick. And we were all laughing. It was a wonderful, approachable, funny, and disarming way to start a conversation with this foundation. We felt instantly bonded through the moment. We didn't get all solemn and embarrassed that the foundation people saw us playing around: we used commonsense charisma to create a shared experience by having some fun.

And yes, they said they loved the visit. I think it's because we just used our charisma and brought our whole, unashamed selves to the interaction. We relaxed and were able to connect by being ourselves.

To me, that is one of the truest ways to demonstrate authentic charisma.

MAKE OTHER PEOPLE FEEL SPECIAL

I never expected to be a teacher. I fell into the classroom thinking it would be temporary, but I absolutely fell in love with the job. I saw that there was a need and found myself dreaming of doing whatever I could to help kids and uplift the profession. I didn't know much that first year of teaching.

But I did have a few big realizations.

I realized that by giving to others, even in little ways, my life seemed to have more meaning. And I realized that a valuable way to give to others was by making them feel appreciated or—even better—special.

I went to a dinner once with a group of people that included Oprah Winfrey. (Okay, now I'm name-dropping.) I was sitting four people down and across the table, but I could see her in the corner of my eye. Whenever the waitstaff came over to her, she would stop them and say things like, "Thank you so much for taking care of us. I appreciate you, and these people mean a lot to me. Thank you for taking care of them." And she would affirm the servers and let them know that their work was appreciated. They were already serving Oprah, so they were already working pretty hard. I mean, everyone loves Oprah. And when you see how she treats people, you understand why.

Once, I witnessed a master class in focusing on someone just a few years after I started teaching. I'll never forget it. Years ago, back when President Clinton was in office, my class was invited to the White House. While everyone was nervously milling around, I went up to the president and said, "President Clinton, the best teacher I've ever met in my life is named Barbara Jones, and she's over there hiding behind that Christmas tree. Would you mind going over there and telling her that you've heard she's great?"

President Clinton smiled and said, "Come with me." We walked over, and the president took Barbara's hands and held them to his chest, saying, "Barbara Jones, I see you, and I'm proud of you and what you do each day."

Everyone in the room watched. Barbara later told me, "He made me feel like the most important person in the world, the way he looked at me, the way he made me feel special."

Successful people make other people feel special. You don't have to be the president. You can make one person—a student, a teacher, a parent—feel special today.

LEAD CALMLY

Imagine you're on a ship, and the captain is guiding the ship, and the waves are going higher and higher, and the boat's surging up and crashing down over and over. You might name the ship *American Education.* You look at the captain, who clutches your arm, saying, "I'm scared. This is horrible!" How would you feel, seeing your captain cowering, frightened, and distraught? You would be absolutely terrified.

But if you look over at the captain and he says, "We'll be okay, I've been here before. We'll get through this storm," his confidence could be life-changing for you in that moment. As an administrator of a school, having positive, confident energy when things are at their worst can right your ship. It can help you set sail stronger, faster, and in more successful ways.

And the converse is also true. If you're a school leader or administrator, and you're having a bad day, and you tell everyone about it, you'll make their day bad as well. Nobody wants to hear that the leader is overwhelmed or stressed. They want to see the leader looking positive and confident that everything's going to be okay.

When I first became an administrator, I realized that when people asked me how I was doing, if I was honest and told them the drama, they would instantly start complaining as well. I took a moment and thought to myself, "Ron, you are going to have to lie every day for the rest of your life."

It may not be fair, but it's true. As the leader, you can't freak out when the waves get high. You can't complain when the seas are rough; you have to invoke confidence, positivity, and strength.

TAKE CARE
OF PEOPLE

Few of us are trapped at sea in life-or-death situations. We live with the smaller stressors, the constant little worries that accumulate in ways that make us impatient, hasty, or rude. We can then become so self-involved that we forget how supporting others brings us joy.

My dad was recently in the hospital. I was staying overnight in the room with him, and his blood pressure alarm began going off. His blood pressure number looked all wrong to me. It was concerning. The red light was flashing.

No one came; no nurses responded. I took off running trying to find them. I ran to the front desk, and I could see a red light flashing at their front desk, too. But three nurses were just sitting there talking and laughing.

"My dad's alarm's going off," I said.

The nurses shrugged. "Uh-huh. Okay, we're coming." But they just sat there.

So I said, "Can you come now, please?"

One of the nurses sort of rolled her eyes and started to turn slowly to leave her chair to come to the room. She said, "There's nothing wrong; I just need to reset the monitor."

I replied, "But if I weren't here, my dad would be lying there help-less with a red light going off. He wouldn't know what was going on. He would be worried!"

She just said, "I honestly don't think he would have even noticed it if you weren't making so much commotion about it."

If the blood pressure monitor had been on me, I would have set off the alarm, too. I wanted to let that nurse have it, but in those situations, you really don't want to upset the person who's responsible for keeping your loved one alive, so I bit my tongue, but I was furious.

I try to remember moments like this when a parent is upset about their child's grades. They feel helpless, too, and in that situation, you and I are the nurses they are turning to for help. It's important for us to reassure people, to calm them down, and to act with urgency to help fix the problem that is causing them so much anxiety.

When I walk through the lobby of RCA, I try to hug all the par-ents, look them in the eyes, and let them know I appreciate them. And when I look at a student, I try to block out everything and not let my eyes dart around the room. I try to focus on the kid.

Focusing on someone else helps me remember the importance of making those important small connections, of looking outside myself to see if there's something I can make better. At RCA, people from all across the country and the world come to watch us teach and learn our methods. I try to use each encounter as a chance for connection.

Sometimes the connection turns out to be surprising. There was a school principal visiting RCA once. I was signing his book, and he said, "Whoa, those are some sharp-stepping shoes, Mr. Clark. What size are they?"

"They're size twelve," I said.

The principal nodded and began joking around. "Oh, I'm size twelve. How about you let me have those shoes? Those shoes are awesome."

I thought, "You know what? You should have them." I popped the shoes off, bent over, picked them up, and handed them to him.

He was pretty taken aback. "Mr. Clark, I can't take these shoes."

"No," I said, "you like them. You should have them." (Honestly, they were a little tight on my feet. I was never going to wear those shoes again. So I just thought, why not?)

Now, I certainly never expected this to happen, but every time that principal wears those shoes, he records himself walking down the hallways of his school. He says, "I'm high stepping today. I'm wearing Ron Clark's shoes." The principal puts those little videos on social media, and they get a lot of traction. I certainly did not give him those shoes to create a social media moment. I just thought, "Oh, he should have the shoes. I don't want to wear them again. He should just have the shoes." But that one percent gesture manifested itself into thousands of views and good PR on social media.

Another time a woman walked into my classroom before a workshop I was about to give, and she was wearing the red T-shirt for one of our school's houses, Amistad. I noticed that she was shivering.

"Oh, are you cold?" I asked.

She smiled. "Yeah. Mr. Clark, you sure keep it chilly in your room."

I looked around and grabbed Mr. Walker, the PE teacher, who was walking by. "Mr. Walker, can you run and grab me a medium red Amistad sweatshirt. I need it now." He took off running because, at our school, people know we prioritize a sense of urgency. If something needs to be done, we might as well do it quickly. So, he hustled.

Right before the workshop started, Mr. Walker ran back into the classroom and handed me the sweatshirt. I walked over and gave it to that woman, who put it on right away. After the workshop, she came up to me and said, "Thank you so much. I can't believe you did that. How much do I owe you?"

I replied, "No, that was a gift from us. It shouldn't be so cold in here." I didn't think much more about it until I saw her leave that day. She was coming out of our school store with two big bags full of Amistad-red merchandise—scarves and sweatshirts. It wasn't the fact that she'd spent money that pleased me so much, it was the fact that she wanted to take her experience at our school home with her.

I shouldn't have been surprised, because when you take care of people and you do what's right, it generally comes back tenfold. Of course, that's not why you should take care of others. It's just right, and you always know when you're doing the right thing.

When you build a community around a culture of kindness, excellence, and making those extra one percent efforts, you learn that what seems small to you in the moment accumulates throughout the day, the week, and the year to build something important. And for those of us privileged enough to be educators, what it all builds is a better future.

MAKE A
CONNECTION

"I'm not going to your school," Zyan said to me as he stood in his apartment's doorway.

"I understand," I said. "That's fine, but could I just come in for a few minutes to meet with you and your mom?"

Zyan just frowned.

Imagine you're in third grade, and you've got loads of friends at your school. Then your parent tells you you're heading to a new school next year, one where you won't know anyone. You are not going to be happy. That's what happens to many kids each year when they hear they are going to attend RCA and start their journey with us as fourth graders. They don't want to leave their friends, and some are really vocal about it. Zyan was one of those kids.

The first time he visited our school, Zyan Wynn straight up told us in about seven ways that he was not coming to our school. Afterward, I called his mom and asked her if he had reconsidered, but she said, "Mr. Clark, it's a lost cause, but I appreciate you trying to help." I asked her if I could visit them, and while she said, "Mr. Clark, this boy is stubborn," she still agreed to let me stop by.

When I arrived, Zyan had his arms crossed. He was frowning and clearly did not want me there. I told him it was okay that he wasn't going to attend RCA, but I asked if I could come inside for a few moments. When I entered, I saw a Connect Four box on the floor.

"Oh, you play Connect Four?" I asked.

Zyan shrugged. "Yes."

"Oh, will you play me? Are you any good?"

"Yes," he said.

We played Connect Four for an hour. After a while, we began chatting. I won every game, and he became more and more frustrated; he kept looking at me like he was asking himself, "How is he doing this?"

After it appeared I had earned some respect in his eyes, I finally asked, "So, Zyan, do you think you might consider coming to our school?"

After a long pause, Zyan said, "I'll come to your school."

As I drove away from their apartment, I was all kinds of emotional. I knew we were going to change his life in profound ways.

Zyan went on to be an outstanding member of RCA. He was the house leader of Amistad, a member of our national championship step team, and Student of the Year. Zyan ended up receiving a full scholarship to a prestigious boarding school, the McCallie School, for high school. You might think that's incredible, but he also received a full scholarship to Princeton and went on to get his master's degree from Harvard. One day Zyan called me and asked, "Mr. Clark, can we go to lunch?" I said sure.

We went to lunch and Zyan said, "Mr. Clark, you know what my master's is in, right?"

"Remind me."

"It's in education." Zyan smiled.

"Oh, that's right," I said. "That's amazing. You want to be a teacher. I love it!"

He said, "Yes, I want to be a teacher. I want to have a Connect Four moment with a student like you had with me."

I fell apart.

And instantly, I hired him.

Zyan Wynn is now a history teacher at RCA. Of all the one percents, maybe taking time to play a Connect Four game will have the biggest impact of them all.

I thought it would be fitting to end this book with the story of Zyan. I don't have any plans to bring my career in education to a close, but we don't live forever, and I definitely see Zyan Wynn as a face of the next generation of teachers. I've spent the last thirty years trying to improve the lives of my students, and I am honored to pass the torch along to Zyan. I know he will outdo my impact by a mile, and I couldn't be more proud to teach alongside Zyan and get to witness this full circle moment firsthand.

Zyan, we need teachers like you. You will be a beacon for others, and I am cheering you on! We all are!

CONCLUSION: SOMETIMES, YOU JUST FUDGE IT

You know the phrase "Close, but no cigar"?

Well, when I was in the sixth grade, I came so close.

My teacher, Mrs. Walker, had nominated me for the gifted program. I had gone through all the testing and whatnot. After it all was over, Mrs. Walker called me out into the hallway and said, "Ron, I want to let you know something. You missed it by one point. You missed the gifted program by just one point."

I sighed. I'd been so close. "Oh, yes ma'am. I'm so sorry." I remember wanting to cry.

Then Mrs. Walker said, "They asked me if you were an all-As student or an As and Bs student. They asked me that because if you make As and Bs, that would earn two extra points. Or if you are a straight-A student, that would get three points. And the truth is that you're an A-B student, Ron. When they added in just the two points, that caused you to miss it. If you were an all-A student, you would have made the program."

"Yes ma'am," I said. I dropped my head, knowing I had let her down.

Then Mrs. Walker looked to the left and the right and leaned in toward me. She whispered, "But I fudged it. I fudged it."

I just stared, not understanding.

"Ron, I fudged it and said you make all As."

"You did?" I asked.

Mrs. Walker nodded and shook my hand. "Now congratulations, Ron. You're in the gifted and talented program, and I have a feeling that you'll never get a B in my class again."

I remember thinking, "I'd be damned. I will never get a B again." The rest of the year I worked so hard, and I never got a B. I made all As. I was so grateful for Mrs. Walker, and she honestly changed the trajectory of my life.

I got a computer in that program—this was in the 1980s when no one had a computer. I got in special classes. I got to go on special field trips. When I went to high school, I was allowed to register for harder classes. I was able to take an online class in high school, which was wild in those days. And I was able to take a tie-in class where I learned Latin thanks to that gifted program.

It changed my entire future.

And it all came from that one moment when she told me, "I fudged it." Sometimes as teachers, maybe we just fudge it. In other words, sometimes we take an extra step to look after kids because that decision could change their lives forever. Sometimes, it may seem like a one percent to us, but to the person you are helping it can be an unimaginable gift.

Sometimes kids need and deserve that little bit of help. You can't do it all the time, of course. Some kids don't work hard enough to deserve it; but in certain cases it's a judgment call. Sometimes it's a call you make because you know it only takes a little tiny bit more to change a life. A tiny bit more. A one percent.

ABOUT RON CLARK

Ron Clark is the *New York Times* bestselling author of *The Essential 55*, which has sold more than one million copies in twenty-five different languages. Clark's other works, *Move Your Bus*, *The End of Molasses Classes*, and *The Excellent 11* were all met with critical acclaim. He has been named American Teacher of the Year by Disney and was Oprah Winfrey's pick as her "Phenomenal Man." He founded the Ron Clark Academy in Atlanta, Georgia, which more than 145,000 educators from around the world have visited to learn about the extraordinary ways that teachers and parents of RCA have helped children achieve great success. Clark has been featured on the *Today* show and CNN, and his experiences have been turned into the uplifting film *The Ron Clark Story*, starring Matthew Perry.

MORE FROM

Since 2012, DBCI has published books that inspire and equip educators to be their best. For more information on our titles or to purchase bulk orders for your school, district, or book study, visit DaveBurgessConsulting.com/DBCIbooks.

The *Like a PIRATE*™ Series
Teach Like a PIRATE by Dave Burgess
eXPlore Like a PIRATE by Michael Matera
Learn Like a PIRATE by Paul Solarz
Plan Like a PIRATE by Dawn M. Harris
Play Like a PIRATE by Quinn Rollins
Run Like a PIRATE by Adam Welcome
Tech Like a PIRATE by Matt Miller

The *Lead Like a PIRATE*™ Series
Lead Like a PIRATE by Shelley Burgess and Beth Houf
Balance Like a PIRATE by Jessica Cabeen, Jessica Johnson, and
    Sarah Johnson
Lead beyond Your Title by Nili Bartley
Lead with Appreciation by Amber Teamann and Melinda Miller
Lead with Collaboration by Allyson Apsey and Jessica Gomez
Lead with Culture by Jay Billy
Lead with Instructional Rounds by Vicki Wilson
Lead with Literacy by Mandy Ellis
She Leads by Dr. Rachael George and Majalise W. Tolan

The EduProtocol Field Guide Series
Deploying EduProtocols by Kim Voge, with Jon Corippo and
    Marlena Hebern

The EduProtocol Field Guide by Marlena Hebern and Jon Corippo
The EduProtocol Field Guide Book 2 by Marlena Hebern and
    Jon Corippo
The EduProtocol Field Guide Math Edition by Lisa Nowakowski and
    Jeremiah Ruesch
The EduProtocol Field Guide Primary Edition by Benjamin Cogswell and
    Jennifer Dean
The EduProtocol Field Guide Social Studies Edition by Dr. Scott M. Petri
    and Adam Moler
The EduProtocol Field Guide ELA Edition by Jacob Carr

Leadership & School Culture
Beyond the Surface of Restorative Practices by Marisol Rerucha
Change the Narrative by Henry J. Turner and Kathy Lopes
Choosing to See by Pamela Seda and Kyndall Brown
Culturize by Jimmy Casas
Discipline Win by Andy Jacks
Educate Me! by Dr. Shree Walker with Micheal D. Ison
Escaping the School Leader's Dunk Tank by Rebecca Coda and
    Rick Jetter
Fight Song by Kim Bearden
From Teacher to Leader by Starr Sackstein
If the Dance Floor Is Empty, Change the Song by Joe Clark
The Innovator's Mindset by George Couros
It's OK to Say "They" by Christy Whittlesey
Kids Deserve It! by Todd Nesloney and Adam Welcome
Leading the Whole Teacher by Allyson Apsey
Let Them Speak by Rebecca Coda and Rick Jetter
The Limitless School by Abe Hege and Adam Dovico
Live Your Excellence by Jimmy Casas
Next-Level Teaching by Jonathan Alsheimer
The Pepper Effect by Sean Gaillard
Principaled by Kate Barker, Kourtney Ferrua, and Rachael George
The Principled Principal by Jeffrey Zoul and Anthony McConnell
Relentless by Hamish Brewer
The Secret Solution by Todd Whitaker, Sam Miller, and Ryan Donlan
Start. Right. Now. by Todd Whitaker, Jeffrey Zoul, and Jimmy Casas

Stop. Right. Now. by Jimmy Casas and Jeffrey Zoul
Teach Your Class Off by CJ Reynolds
Teachers Deserve It by Rae Hughart and Adam Welcome
They Call Me "Mr. De" by Frank DeAngelis
Thrive through the Five by Jill M. Siler
Unmapped Potential by Julie Hasson and Missy Lennard
When Kids Lead by Todd Nesloney and Adam Dovico
Word Shift by Joy Kirr
Your School Rocks by Ryan McLane and Eric Lowe

Technology & Tools
50 Things to Go Further with Google Classroom by Alice Keeler and Libbi Miller
50 Things You Can Do with Google Classroom by Alice Keeler and Libbi Miller
50 Ways to Engage Students with Google Apps by Alice Keeler and Heather Lyon
140 Twitter Tips for Educators by Brad Currie, Billy Krakower, and Scott Rocco
Block Breaker by Brian Aspinall
Building Blocks for Tiny Techies by Jamila "Mia" Leonard
Code Breaker by Brian Aspinall
The Complete EdTech Coach by Katherine Goyette and Adam Juarez
Control Alt Achieve by Eric Curts
The Esports Education Playbook by Chris Aviles, Steve Isaacs, Christine Lion-Bailey, and Jesse Lubinsky
Google Apps for Littles by Christine Pinto and Alice Keeler
Master the Media by Julie Smith
Raising Digital Leaders by Jennifer Casa-Todd
Reality Bytes by Christine Lion-Bailey, Jesse Lubinsky, and Micah Shippee, PhD
Sail the 7 Cs with Microsoft Education by Becky Keene and Kathi Kersznowski
Shake Up Learning by Kasey Bell
Social LEADia by Jennifer Casa-Todd
Stepping Up to Google Classroom by Alice Keeler and Kimberly Mattina
Teaching Math with Google Apps by Alice Keeler and Diana Herrington

Teaching with Google Jamboard by Alice Keeler and Kimberly Mattina
Teachingland by Amanda Fox and Mary Ellen Weeks

Teaching Methods & Materials
All 4s and 5s by Andrew Sharos
Boredom Busters by Katie Powell
Building Strong Writers by Christina Schneider
The Classroom Chef by John Stevens and Matt Vaudrey
The Collaborative Classroom by Trevor Muir
Copyrighteous by Diana Gill
CREATE by Bethany J. Petty
Ditch That Homework by Matt Miller and Alice Keeler
Ditch That Textbook by Matt Miller
Don't Ditch That Tech by Matt Miller, Nate Ridgway, and Angelia Ridgway
EDrenaline Rush by John Meehan
Educated by Design by Michael Cohen, The Tech Rabbi
Empowered to Choose: A Practical Guide to Personalized Learning by Andrew Easton
Expedition Science by Becky Schnekser
Frustration Busters by Katie Powell
Fully Engaged by Michael Matera and John Meehan
Game On? Brain On! by Lindsay Portnoy, PhD
Guided Math AMPED by Reagan Tunstall
Happy & Resilient by Roni Habib
Innovating Play by Jessica LaBar-Twomy and Christine Pinto
Instant Relevance by Denis Sheeran
Instructional Coaching Connection by Nathan Lang-Raad
Keeping the Wonder by Jenna Copper, Ashley Bible, Abby Gross, and Staci Lamb
LAUNCH by John Spencer and A.J. Juliani
Learning in the Zone by Dr. Sonny Magana
Lights, Cameras, TEACH! by Kevin J. Butler
Make Learning MAGICAL by Tisha Richmond
Pass the Baton by Kathryn Finch and Theresa Hoover
Project-Based Learning Anywhere by Lori Elliott
Pure Genius by Don Wettrick
The Revolution by Darren Ellwein and Derek McCoy

The Science Box by Kim Adsit and Adam Peterson
Shift This! by Joy Kirr
Skyrocket Your Teacher Coaching by Michael Cary Sonbert
Spark Learning by Ramsey Musallam
Sparks in the Dark by Travis Crowder and Todd Nesloney
Table Talk Math by John Stevens
Teachables by Cheryl Abla and Lisa Maxfield
Unpack Your Impact by Naomi O'Brien and LaNesha Tabb
The Wild Card by Hope and Wade King
Writefully Empowered by Jacob Chastain
The Writing on the Classroom Wall by Steve Wyborney
You Are Poetry by Mike Johnston
You'll Never Guess What I'm Saying by Naomi O'Brien
You'll Never Guess What I'm Thinking About by Naomi O'Brien

Inspiration, Professional Growth & Personal Development
Be REAL by Tara Martin
Be the One for Kids by Ryan Sheehy
The Coach ADVenture by Amy Illingworth
Creatively Productive by Lisa Johnson
The Ed Branding Book by Dr. Renae Bryant and Lynette White
Educational Eye Exam by Alicia Ray
The EduNinja Mindset by Jennifer Burdis
Empower Our Girls by Lynmara Colón and Adam Welcome
Finding Lifelines by Andrew Grieve and Andrew Sharos
The Four O'Clock Faculty by Rich Czyz
How Much Water Do We Have? by Pete and Kris Nunweiler
P Is for Pirate by Dave and Shelley Burgess
A Passion for Kindness by Tamara Letter
The Path to Serendipity by Allyson Apsey
PheMOMenal Teacher by Annick Rauch
Recipes for Resilience by Robert A. Martinez
Rogue Leader by Rich Czyz
Sanctuaries by Dan Tricarico
Saving Sycamore by Molly B. Hudgens
The Secret Sauce by Rich Czyz
Shattering the Perfect Teacher Myth by Aaron Hogan

Stories from Webb by Todd Nesloney

Talk to Me by Kim Bearden

Teach Better by Chad Ostrowski, Tiffany Ott, Rae Hughart, and Jeff Gargas

Teach Me, Teacher by Jacob Chastain

Teach, Play, Learn! by Adam Peterson

The Teachers of Oz by Herbie Raad and Nathan Lang-Raad

TeamMakers by Laura Robb and Evan Robb

Through the Lens of Serendipity by Allyson Apsey

Write Here and Now by Dan Tricarico

The Zen Teacher by Dan Tricarico

Children's Books

The Adventures of Little Mickey by Mickey Smith Jr.

Alpert by LaNesha Tabb

Alpert & Friends by LaNesha Tabb

Beyond Us by Aaron Polansky

Cannonball In by Tara Martin

Dolphins in Trees by Aaron Polansky

Dragon Smart by Tisha and Tommy Richmond

I Can Achieve Anything by MoNique Waters

I Want to Be a Lot by Ashley Savage

The Magic of Wonder by Jenna Copper, Ashley Bible, Abby Gross, and Staci Lamb

Micah's Big Question by Naomi O'Brien

The Princes of Serendip by Allyson Apsey

Ride with Emilio by Richard Nares

A Teacher's Top Secret Confidential by LaNesha Tabb

A Teacher's Top Secret: Mission Accomplished by LaNesha Tabb

The Wild Card Kids by Hope and Wade King

Zom-Be a Design Thinker by Amanda Fox